MARTELLO TOWERS

MARTELLO

Sheila Sutcliffe

David & Charles · Newton Abbot

TOWERS

ISBN 0 7153 5607 0

Set in 11/13 Baskerville
and printed in Great Britain
by W. J. Holman Limited Dawlish
for David & Charles (Publishers) Limited
South Devon House Newton Abbot Devon

To Holman, John and Charles

CONTENTS

LIST OF ILLUSTRATIONS

page

PLATES

page

IN TEXT

PREFACE

This book is the result of the research which I began soon after the highly individual martello tower at Aldeburgh in Suffolk had caught my attention and prompted me to discover more about the history and origin of these buildings for my own interest. It soon became evident that there was nothing readily available on the subject. There are some local newspaper and magazine articles on particular towers or groups of them in a limited area, but no larger all-embracing review or history has been undertaken, with one notable exception. This was an article by the late Commander Hilary P. Mead, RN, which appeared in 1948 in *The Mariner's Mirror* (the Journal of the Society of Nautical Research) on the martello towers of England. For this valuable survey, Commander Mead visited all the existing towers in England, apart from three in Suffolk where deep shingle made it impossible. Having referred in his article to the sites of the martellos, the condition of the surviving towers and their varied uses, he made tempting references to the fact that others were to be found elsewhere in the world, a remark that opened fresh avenues of research for me.

In England, where martellos were more numerous than anywhere else, the squat, circular buildings, sombre and forbidding, have been part of the seaside environment for generations of holidaymakers, along with seagulls, boats and buckets and spades. They were part of my own background. I made sandcastles in their likeness beneath the Wish Tower at Eastbourne, watched flights of swallows arriving for the summer in the shelter of a Pevensey Bay martello and ran barefoot over the sandy drawbridge to drink ginger beer in the dank gloom of the one at Seaford. Despite these experiences I had, like most people, only a cursory knowledge of their history, and they have been slow to give up their secrets. Sir Walter Scott's description of them in *Peveril of the Peak,* written only a few years after they were built, is as true today as it was then; the towers were '. . . built . . . in such a fashion as if . . . intended . . . , as an Irishman said of the Martello Towers, for the sole purpose of puzzling posterity'. Perhaps these findings will help to solve the riddle.

CHAPTER ONE

INTRODUCTION

Among the many fortifications built over the centuries for coastal defence, the most historically interesting and architecturally curious are the martello towers. Solid, low and circular, they were massively built of stone or stuccoed brick with guns mounted on the flat roof. Their purpose was to provide concentrated fire on ships at sea to repel an enemy landing, and they were capable of withstanding a siege of considerable duration. The towers were strategically placed to protect coastal batteries, vital installations and any particularly vulnerable stretch of coast where an invasion might be expected. They were, in fact, considered to be buttresses of the 'wooden walls'—the name by which warships were then known. Their amphibious nature was not confined to their site alone, but applied also to their whole concept, for they were designed by army engineers to be manned by the artillery in support of, or in place of, the navy. Martello towers were conceived and first constructed by the British during the long war with France that lasted almost continuously from 1793 to 1815.

The classic period for martello building was the Napoleonic era and the towers are best known and most frequent on the south coast of England nearest to the Continent of Europe. However, their distribution was extensive, and while their greatest concentration was in Britain (including Ireland, Jersey and the Orkneys), they were also built in the then British colonies of Canada and South Africa, as well as in the United States of America. The span of time during which they were built was considerable: three-quarters of a century lay between the construction of the first two towers in South Africa in 1796 and the termination of the uncompleted work on the last two at Key West in the United States.

This wide range in space and time led inevitably to some variation in design, but however much the martellos may

The countries where martello towers were built

Page 17 The tower at St Fiorenzo Bay, Corsica, at the time of the battle in 1794. Aquatint by J. T. Lee and T. Hall, published in 1809

Page 18 Mortella Tower, Corsica. One of two watercolour sketches painted soon after the action by the British fleet in 1794 by a member of the services with the initials CFD

differ in detail, they have one essential characteristic in common, a feature linking them with the earliest masonry fortifications to be built: a single entrance doorway placed high above ground level so that attackers would find the building almost impossible to enter. The only means of reaching the door was by a movable ladder or rope which could be pulled up into the building after use. This primitive form of defence can be traced from the ancient watch-towers of the Mediterranean—many of which were built by the Phoenicians—to the keeps of early Norman castles, by which time the movable ladder had been replaced by a wooden staircase that could be easily destroyed in the event of an attack.

Mediterranean watch-towers, the direct ancestors of martello towers, can still be seen, standing boldly and romantically on the skyline on rocky cliffs and headlands or above the curve of some inviting bay. They were built during successive centuries from prehistoric times and their purpose was to give warning to the local inhabitants of the approach of pirates intent on raiding for loot and slaves. It was for this reason that at one time they were called generically Corsair (pirate) or Saracen (infidel) towers. A warning signal—usually a fire lit on the tower's flat roof—for people to seek cover in the surrounding country was given by a lookout as soon as he saw an enemy or unidentified ship approaching.[1] The watch-towers are more numerous in the western basin of the Mediterranean, especially on the islands, the shores of which were for centuries the happy hunting ground of the dreaded Barbary Coast pirates and the main source of their galley slaves.

It was, however, one particular tower that was the inspiration of martellos, and ironically it was one on the island of Corsica, the birthplace of Napoleon Bonaparte himself. A single incident of naval warfare led to the adoption of this form of defence which, as every fresh emergency arose, seemed to be the answer to the particular dilemma for three-quarters of a century.[2] During the first year of the war between France and Britain, an appeal came from the leader of the Corsican patriots, a man named General Paoli who was well known in London, for help to free them from the French revolutionary forces which were occupying the island. The French troops were concentrated in the north of the island at San Fiorenzo, Calvi and Bastia, and in September 1793 British ships were sent to blockade these ports and at the same time to secure a safe anchorage for future operations. Such an anchorage was found in the Gulf of San Fiorenzo, from which access could be gained to all three towns. In the approaches to San Fiorenzo were three ancient watch-towers, armed and manned by the French; of these, the capture of the one on Mortella Point was vital if the town were to be taken. It was therefore bombarded by HMS *Lowestoft*, and surrendered after about two hours' firing. A garrison of Corsican patriots was then installed, but their words were braver than their deeds, and within a short time the tower was recaptured by the French.

The second attack on the tower came in February of the next year, when Lord Hood and the fleet sailed into the gulf and prepared to capture the island. The first task was to retake the tower on Mortella Point, and HMS *Fortitude* (74 guns) and HMS *Juno* (32 guns) began to attack it. They were, however, repulsed and forced to withdraw with serious damage and sixty casualties, including six killed. It was then left to the army, which had already landed further along the coast, to besiege the tower. This they did after Major-General David Dundas and Lieutenant-General John Moore had raised a battery of four guns 150 yards from it. Even then it took two days of heavy and continuous firing before the tower was surrendered, and in the end this was mainly due to a fire in some rubbish that had been built into the parapet with other material to strengthen it on the seaward side. Both naval and military officers were deeply impressed by this resistance, especially as the garrison consisted of thirty-eight men and the armament was only one 6-pounder and two 18-pounder guns.

The Mortella Point tower was, in fact, the key to the whole island, and although there was some heavy fighting still to come, the British eventually occupied it and gained a valuable base.

This engagement gave military architects a new type of fortification, and caused officers to ponder on the principle that coastal defence by towers with a very few guns could repel ships at sea armed with many guns. A number of the officers present at this action later held important posts in England and influenced the adoption of the martello scheme for the Kent and Sussex coasts, as well as the design of the tower. They included Vice-Admiral Sir John Jervis, Rear-Admiral George Elphinstone, Major-General David Dundas, Colonel Abraham D'Aubant, Lieutenant-Colonel Thomas Nepean and Lieutenant-Colonel John Moore—better known as Sir John Moore, the hero of Corunna.

At the same time, a new word was added to the English language. The corruption of the word Mortella by the transposition of the first and last vowel may seem strange, but British servicemen have always been adept at twisting foreign place names to suit their tongues. There was also an easily understandable confusion with the name given to these watch-towers in parts of western Italy. On the shores of the Roman Campagna and the offshore islands they were usually known as 'torri di martello', indicating that the alarm was raised by striking a bell with a hammer (*martello*) rather than by lighting a fire. As Lord Hood and the Mediterranean fleet came straight to Corsica from one of these Italian island, Elba, the resultant word with a compound meaning is not surprising. From contemporary despatches and letters, it is clear that several versions of the word were in use before it settled down to its familiar form. One naval officer wrote home about 'Myrtello Point', which showed he had grasped the significance of the geographical name, for the headland on which the tower stood was covered with a dense mass of wild myrtle. The name martello seems to have been the popular one in the navy, but it was not universally accepted at first. The buildings were usually referred to simply as 'the towers', 'sea-towers' or 'towers as sea-batteries'; but when they were under discussion in 1804, the army called them 'bomb-proof towers', while in Parliament they were spoken of as 'Corsican towers' and for the first time in 1803 as 'martello towers'. But the name derived from the tower at Mortella Point was destined to live longer than the building itself. In the autumn of 1796 the British found it expedient to withdraw from the whole of the Mediterranean, and Corsica was evacuated. In order that it would never again cause them any trouble, the Mortella Point tower was blown up—not without difficulty, its walls being 15ft thick. Fortunately, some records were made of it before this irrevocable step was taken. Soon after the tower capitulated for the first time, some delightful pen and water-colour drawings were made of the exterior of the tower, and the layout of the armament on the roof, by an amateur artist with the initials C.F.D. These drawings are preserved in the National Maritime Museum at Greenwich, London. Lord Hood's secretary, John McArthur, later had a carefully drawn version of them engraved, and a Captain Pakenham made a wooden model of the tower in two hinged sections, showing both interior and exterior. This was presented to the Royal Artillery by the Commander-in-Chief of the Mediterranean, Admiral Sir John Jervis, and it is held by them in the Rotunda at their Institution at Woolwich, London. It was this same admiral who wrote prophetically, but with complete disregard of syntax, '. . . I hope to see such works erected . . . on every part of the coast likely for an enemy to make a descent on'.

A few months before this, the first two descendants of the Mortella Point tower were built in South Africa at Cape Colony, a Dutch settlement seized by the British in 1795. New defences were built in preparation for an expected counter-attack and among these were two small round towers. This was hardly surprising as the man who led the expedition and became the first British governor of Cape Colony was George Elphinstone—now Vice-Admiral—who had been with the Mediterranean fleet off Corsica the previous year. A little later in the same year that the towers at Cape Town and Simon's Town were built (1796) one was begun at Halifax, Nova Scotia. Although it was inspired by the much-discussed prototype in Corsica, it failed in several ways to measure up to it in construction.

Between 1796 and the end of the war in 1815, 194 towers were built—all, with the exception of the early ones in Cape Colony and Halifax, to recognised standards—as part of a comprehensive defence scheme, and as a direct result of Great Britain's war with France and her ally, the United States of America. From 1815 the vogue for martello building in Europe was over, with the exception of Jersey where five more towers were built. The construction of martellos was henceforth confined to North America, where defensive measures were kept alive by the political tension existing between Britain and the United States. Between 1820 and 1870 America built six martellos among her new coastal fortifications, while Canada added five to her existing number.

Martello building came to an end in 1873 with the abandonment of the Key West project in Florida; work was stopped on the two unfinished towers known as martellos. Owing to their vast size and complicated construction they are almost in a class apart, although the central tower retained the characteristic high-level entrance door, flat roof and vaulted chambers. It was, however, a far cry from the simple little tower at Mortella Point in Corsica. And so, not with a salute of guns, but, as it were, with a damp squib, the martello epoch was over. The towers were obsolete: improved artillery and ironclad ships had made them a complete anachronism. Undoubtedly, they could have given a good account of themselves at the beginning of the century, but they were never put to the test. They must have had some psychological effect on would-be attackers, for the French nicknamed them 'bulldogs', showing they realised that martellos were characteristic in every way of Britain's determination to resist invasion. In England they have more recently been described as the 'Bluestreak of the Napoleonic era'. At least they were not the Maginot line.

Many martello towers are still standing. Seafaring men are familiar with them and they are part of the marine environment. Wind and weather, neglect and coastal erosion have swept some away; others have fallen victim to the march of progress and have been cleared away for buildings of a more practical nature. In England, some disappeared when the seashore was turned into the seaside and fishing villages became holiday resorts, fed by a network of railways from London. Forty-three survive of the original 103. Of those that remain, some are in a sad state of disrepair and decay, abandoned in undignified surroundings. There has, however, been a movement, starting in Canada and spreading slowly to the United States, South Africa, Ireland and England, to befriend and preserve a few of the martello towers before it is too late.

Notes on this chapter appear on page 163

CHAPTER TWO

THE HISTORICAL CONTEXT

The end of the eighteenth century found Europe in a state of turmoil. Revolution in France had sparked off a war which was not finally resolved until the battle of Waterloo in 1815. It proved to be a war fought on many fronts and over an astonishingly wide area, with great powers and lesser ones all drawn into the net. Allies might come and go, coalitions be formed only to disintegrate, but the two main contestants, France and Britain, carried on to the bitter end, the one supreme on land, the other at sea. For more than twenty years men of the British army were scattered about the world as distant countries became involved, while the navy was constantly employed patrolling the seas, blockading enemy ports, transporting troops and convoying merchantmen as well as engaging the enemy whenever their paths crossed. Control of the sea was vital and the naval battles that culminated in Nelson's victory at Trafalgar put the seal on Britain's supremacy. Her continued maintenance of sea power and control of communications gave her immunity from invasion, and for the whole of the war Britain sheltered behind her 'wooden walls'.

From the outbreak of the French Revolution in 1789 it had been obvious that a country such as Britain, with a monarchical system of government, could not avoid a clash with a neighbour of such widely differing ideals. Britain's hatred of revolutionary policies became panic at the onset of the Reign of Terror in France, and there was growing concern over a small but vociferous minority in Britain whose subversive activities and direct contact with the French government was causing alarm. Finally, when the rabble in arms that went by the name of the French Revolutionary Army invaded the Austrian Netherlands and made rapid progress towards Holland, the stage was set for a confrontation. Britain had long maintained that the Low Countries—because of their geographical position in relation to the Channel seaways and Britain's coast—should be in the hands of friendly powers. She rightly feared that large numbers of small boats might be concealed in the maze of inland waterways ready for an invasion. And so in 1793, not for the first time nor the last, Britain went to war because of the situation in the Low Countries. Within a short time, France had overrun the Netherlands, and Holland became the Batavian Republic and France's vassal state. The remnants of the British troops limped ignominiously home, their mission unfulfilled.

Britain's performance on land during the first years of the war gave little cause for celebration or hope of glory and an early victory. The Netherlands fiasco was followed by disaster in the West Indies and fruitless raids to support French royalist risings in Europe. The few successes that could be claimed were almost entirely due to naval co-operation. These included the occupation of Corsica in 1794 and the annexation of the Dutch colony of the Cape of Good Hope in the following year, both of which have an important bearing on the study of martello towers. The Cape of Good Hope venture was the most worthwhile and far-sighted action of the period. It was either a stroke of good luck or genius that caused Pitt and his colleagues to appreciate the significance of this trading post on the sea route to India and the Far East. Its far-reaching consequences affected not only the course of the war but British history, and its political importance is recognised to the present day.

Britain's victories during this period were won at sea. As an island nation, the strength of her navy was of paramount importance and the key to her defence. For most of the war France had as allies the important maritime powers of Holland and Spain; their combined fleets were far superior to Britain's in numbers. But the British policy of blockading enemy naval bases prevented them from joining forces and her seamanship and superior strategy more than compensated for the discrepancy in numbers.

As the century drew to a close and young Napoleon Bonaparte achieved fame, first by his military exploits and then by his political leadership, it was he who was regarded as Britain's enemy, and the war of opinions that had followed the revolution drifted imperceptibly into a war against a despot's claim to worldwide domination. It was not for nothing that he earned himself the title of Boney, the Bogeyman of Europe.

A state of stalemate was reached by 1802, and a truce was called with the Treaty of Amiens. The peace was short-lived and unsatisfactory, and war was resumed in the following year. Britain stood alone, her adversary's invincible army ranged against her on the other side of the English Channel. For over two years from May 1803 the invasion of England was Napoleon's consuming passion, to which he devoted all his energies and those of his country. 'The Channel is but a ditch' he boasted, 'and anyone may cross it who has the courage.' His goal was the capital and his aim to raise his standard over the Tower of London.

Napoleon's plan to invade England was not original. It had long been part of the French tradition of warfare against the British Isles, and soon after war broke out invasion plans were revived. The idea Napoleon inherited was to build and assemble a fleet of flat-bottomed boats in the Channel ports and to throw a vast army on to the English coast somewhere between Dover and Hastings. Before his first contemplated invasion in 1798, a number of landings were threatened and two actually took place. They were not connected with the Channel ports invasion flotilla and were planned as demoralising raids directed at the fringes of the kingdom, to act as feints and draw forces away from protecting more vital parts of the country. Some of these attempts never got further than the harbour mouth because of the blockade; others were blown off course in bad weather and some were becalmed. Of those which succeeded, there was the comic opera landing of a gang of convicts at Fishguard in Wales in 1797 who were routed by the local militia.

It was against Ireland, however, that the French concentrated their efforts, and here was the chink in Britain's armour. A Catholic country, chafing under English rule and dreaming of independence, the discontented population was ripe for rebellion and in constant touch with the French government, who confidently expected local support when their troops landed. But when open rebellion finally broke out in Ireland in 1798, it was so savagely put down by the government that the promised uprisings that should have coincided with a French landing at Killala Bay in County Mayo a few months later were not forthcoming. Nevertheless, French troops fought on Irish soil for almost three weeks before they surrendered. It was hardly surprising, therefore, that when martello towers were recognised as a proper form of coastal defence, the first place that they were built, a year before any were started in England, was Ireland.

Napoleon made ready for his onslaught on the Channel coast of England on three separate occasions. The first two, in 1798 and 1801, have sometimes been considered merely as diplomatic moves. His third attempt from 1803 to 1805 was different. The scale on which it was designed and the vigour with which he organised the preparations put it in a class apart from anything that had gone before. His plan succeeded in turning England into an armed camp and led to the building of the martello towers. Boulogne was the centre of operations, and his army, known since 1801 as the Army of England, camped on the cliffs above the town. Here, within sight and sound of the English coast, some 130,000 men paraded and rehearsed their embarkation drill, waiting for the signal that never came. Meanwhile, the shipyards of the Channel ports and those of the canals of the Low Countries rang to the sound of hammers. All manner of flat-bottomed boats were produced, equipped for men, guns, horses and fodder, until the flotilla at Boulogne and in the neighbouring ports numbered 2,240 vessels.

So confident was Napoleon of his success, that he had a medal struck to commemorate the landing on English soil. One side bore his classic, laurel-wreathed head, the other a representation of England as Neptune being crushed in the arms of a godlike young man, the symbol of France. The inscription read, optimistically, 'Descente en Angleterre' and, to add insult to injury, 'Frappé à Londres, 1804'.

While Napoleon was amassing the Boulogne flotilla, he had to devise a way of conducting it safely across the Channel. For this he had various ideas. His first was to build sufficient flat-bottomed gunboats to shoot a way through the lines of British battleships. An equally impracticable scheme was to rely on the cover of darkness or fog to make a surprise landing. But the flotilla was unseaworthy in winter, and summer nights are short, and fog unpredictable. Neither night nor fog would have been long enough to make the crossing possible, for it was calculated that it would take six days to move all the unwieldy craft out of harbour and into clear water before the journey began. There was no hope of bringing up the French battleships to escort the flotilla for, by an unkind trick of geography, the harbours that could accommodate them were to the west at the naval bases of Brest and Rochefort, and the blockade and patrolling battleships at the entrance to the Channel made the manoeuvre impossible. In the end Napoleon realised that his only chance was to clear the Channel of British ships by drawing them off on a wild goose chase—the French fleet doubling back to hold the Channel while the crossing was effected. The result of this line of thought was the dash across the Atlantic by the French fleet under Admiral Villeneuve in 1805, with Nelson in hot pursuit. It produced the most decisive battle of the war, which was the direct result of Napoleon's attempted invasion of England.

This chase was the curtain-raiser to the battle of Trafalgar. What appeared to be a marauding expedition against the British West Indian sugar plantations was in reality Napoleon's last desperate bid to get the invasion under way. But his strategy miscarried. Nelson, angered that the French had slipped through his Mediterranean blockade, hunted them across the Atlantic and, instead of lingering among the islands looking for the enemy as was expected, chased them all the way back again. Hard pressed and cut off from making his way into the Channel to carry out the main part of his mission, Villeneuve and his ships sought refuge in Spanish ports, while Napoleon waited in vain at Boulogne. By the middle of August, he wrote hopefully to Villeneuve, cooped up behind the British blockade in Cadiz, 'We are ready everywhere. Your presence in the Channel for twenty-four hours will suffice.' After waiting a week, Napoleon realised that his admiral would never come, and gave orders for the Army of England to march against Austria. When he commanded his fleet to leave Cadiz and move into the Mediterranean, it emerged to be met by the waiting Nelson, who closed in for the kill at Trafalgar.

The whole operation had been a gigantic miscalculation by a land commander. Any thought of invasion was over. If it had ever been a possibility, Napoleon had lost his chance. He turned his back on the tempting shores of England and began a series of victorious battles to compensate for the wasted years and frustration of the Boulogne camp. During the next ten years, the Army of England was dissipated across the face of Europe, while the invasion flotilla rotted along the Channel coast and the martello towers continued to be built on the British side.

An unforseen consequence of the failure of the invasion plan was the entrance of the United States of America into the war as an unexpected ally of France. Napoleon, incensed by his failure to conquer Britain, determined to break the island of shopkeepers by cutting off their lifeline of overseas trade, made possible by Britain's continued control of the sea. By a series of ordinances which became known collectively as the Continental System, Napoleon decreed that none of his vassal states was to import British goods. Britain was quick to retaliate, and imposed an even stronger blockade on all ports to stop any goods from entering the Continent. This angered the United States which had remained neutral and traded freely with Europe. Added to this severe treatment, US ships had suffered for some time from the practise of British sea captains who stopped and searched neutral vessels in case they carried any British naval deserters. For both these reasons, and too late to make any appreciable difference to the outcome of the war, America joined in the fray in 1812.

For the first time since 1805, Britain's superiority at sea was challenged in a series of single-ship contests by the Americans. This interlude did not last long. In a matter of months the American ports were blockaded with most of their ships inside, and the British fleet was able to sail safely in American waters, and land and raid at will. Because of the initial American successes and their far-ranging fast frigates, two martellos were built in the Orkneys off the north coast of Scotland, where convoys gathered before crossing the Atlantic, while towers were added on the north coast of Ireland at Lough Foyle and Lough Swilly. At the same time, since most of America's efforts were naturally directed against Canada, two towers were added on her Atlantic coast. Ironically, the Treaty of Ghent, which brought peace to the two nations in 1814, sowed the seed for further antagonism which almost led to a clash of arms thirty years later, and brought about the building of martellos at Kingston on Lake Ontario.

There were signs that Napoleon's power was beginning to wane by the time America came into the war. The fighting in Spain was slowly sapping his empire's strength on one front, and on the other the Russian campaign had ended in the disastrous retreat from Moscow. The peace of 1814 was all too brief and it was not until Wellington had routed Napoleon at Waterloo as thoroughly as Nelson had done ten years previously at Trafalgar that the war was really over.

CHAPTER THREE

THE EVOLUTION OF THE MARTELLO TOWER DESIGN

The dimensions and style of the Mediterranean watch-towers did not conform to any set pattern because they were built by widely separated communities over successive centuries. All of them, however, had the essential characteristics that had impressed the British forces in their engagement against the tower at Mortella Point which became the prototype of all martello towers. These were massive walls, a flat roof and the important high-level entrance door. The height of the door above the surrounding ground was between 10ft and 20ft. It was calculated by assuming that one man stood on another's shoulders with arms stretched upwards as if reaching for the door sill; to this measurement a few feet were sometimes added as a margin of safety. Records differ as to the dimensions of the Mortella Point tower, but they are usually considered to have been as follows:

height	40ft
base diameter	45ft
thickness of walls	15ft

Towers as a means of coastal defence had fallen out of use in northern Europe from the end of the Middle Ages because of the development of artillery power. It was not until Britain was faced with the prospect of an unfamiliar type of warfare, namely enemy landings from small craft in waters where battleships dared not venture, that the idea of towers was considered. Their worth and effectiveness in this sort of fighting had been proved over many centuries in the Mediterranean and the British army and navy were acquainted with them from service in that area. The army was also accustomed to ordnance towers which, though not common, were built during the latter part of the eighteenth century. Instances of small, circular, detatched coastal towers being built before the classic martello age began are of interest in showing not only that the idea was being gradually accepted, but also the development of certain features found in the eventual martello design.

The beginning of this early movement towards towers is seen in a series of them constructed in the Channel Isles late in the eighteenth century. This group of islands, consisting of Guernsey, Jersey, Alderney and Sark, is situated uncomfortably close to the shores of France, in much the same position with regard to raids as the Mediterranean islands were to their mainland neighbours. Their coasts were dotted with fortifications of all sorts, built at various times, and after 1778 a series of round towers was added to this collection, first in Jersey and shortly afterwards in Guernsey. The design of the towers differed between the two islands, but they had features in common and bore a marked resemblance to Mediterranean watch-towers, which must have been their inspiration, although as yet no definite attribution has been established nor have plans of the buildings been discovered in either case. In both islands the towers have become known as martellos, a misnomer which has led to much confusion.[1] Their purpose was similar to that of a martello but they were planned before the Mortella Point incident took place in 1794 and they lack some of the necessary characteristics.

In Jersey, each tower was originally called simply 'La tour', followed frequently by the name of the place where it was

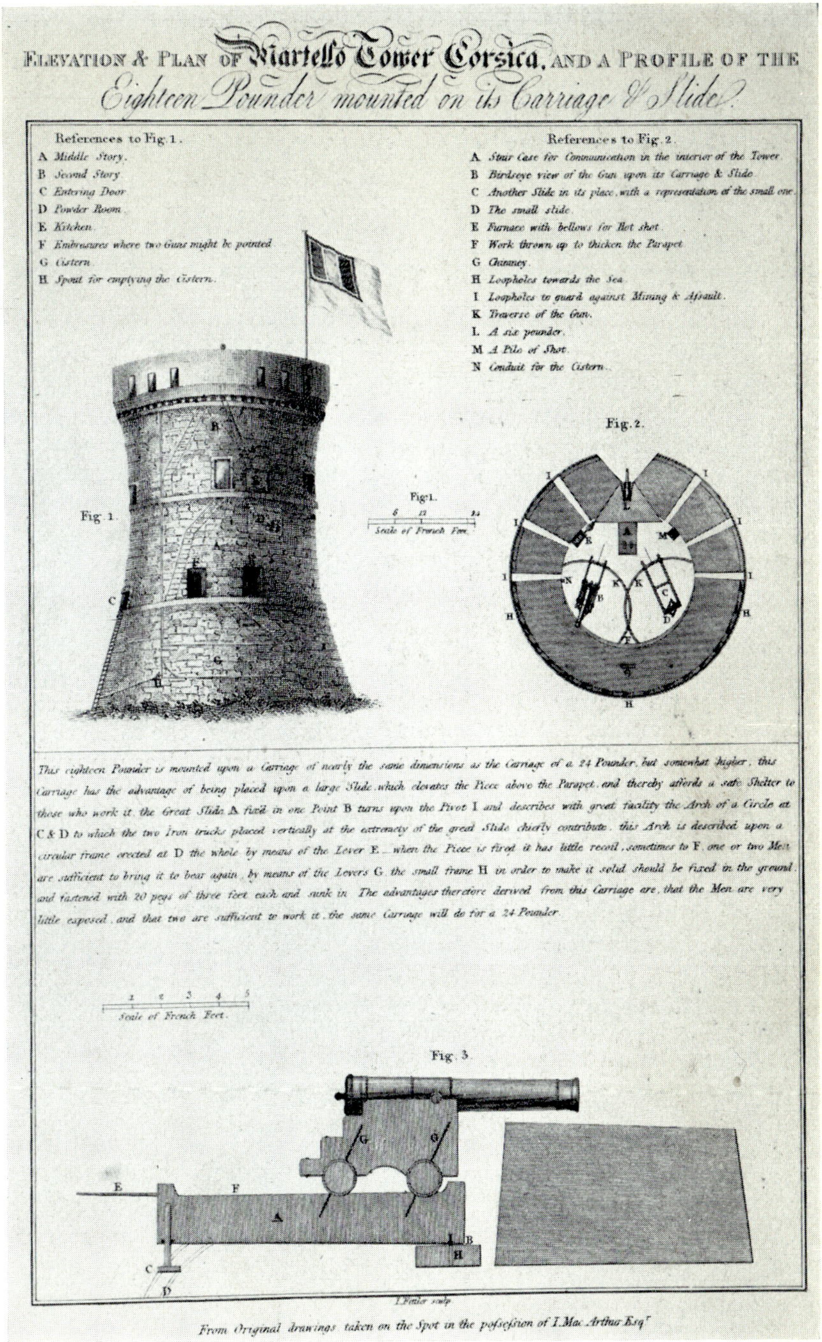

Page 35 Elevation and plan of Mortella Tower, Corsica; an engraving based on the original drawings then in the possession of J. MacArthur, Secretary to Lord Hood

Page 36 (above) The interior of the Mortella tower. The hinged wooden model made by Captain Pakenham before the tower was destroyed, and presented to the Royal Artillery. Measurements when closed, base diameter 11$\frac{3}{4}$in, height 14$\frac{7}{8}$in; *(below)* tower at Le Hocq, Jersey, one of the coastal towers built in the Channel Isles before the Mortella Point action

situated—or, in military style, by a number. They were certainly thought of as martellos by 1830, for in that year King William IV asked his aide-de-camp in Jersey, Sir John Le Couteur, whether there were any martellos in the bays of his island. Sir John replied 'Yes, Sir, four, three, two and one in the accessible bays in proportion to their extent'. As only three martellos were built there during the Napoleonic wars, it is obvious he was referring to the other towers as well.

It was General Henry Conway, Governor of Jersey and previously Lieutenant-General of Ordnance, who in 1778 proposed that thirty round towers should be built on the island's coasts. Extra protection was needed to repel expected French raids because war had broken out once more between Britain and her traditional enemy, this time as a result of the American War of Independence. Building began in 1779 and by 1794—the year of the Mortella Point incident—twenty had been completed. One of these, Seymour Tower, for no apparent reason was square, but the remainder were round. La Rocca, the final tower, was not begun until 1796. The work hung fire because of lack of money, but it was finished by 1801. The officer responsible for obtaining the necessary money and getting the work started again was Lieutenant-Colonel Benjamin Fisher, then Commanding Royal Engineer in Jersey. Later he was to hold the same post in Ireland when martellos were built there, and it is more than probable that he was partly responsible for their design.

The Jersey towers were of stone, and the walls were pierced at frequent intervals by large loopholes or *créneaux* for firing through—a practice frowned upon by the designers of the English martellos because it weakened the walls.[2] The dimensions were:

height	36ft
base diameter	34ft
thickness of walls at base	8ft
decreasing to	6ft at the crest[3]

With regard to the eventual martello tower design, these towers had two interesting features. The walls had a distinct slope or batter from the base of the building to the crest. This device, for throwing off a glancing shot from a ship at sea, was used in most martellos and gave them their characteristic 'upturned flower-pot' profile. Also, projecting from the parapet round the flat roof were four machicolated galleries, a form of defence used in the Irish martellos and in some of the ones in North America. They were introduced in the Sherbrooke Tower at Halifax, Nova Scotia, which was begun in 1814. When the Prince of Wales' Tower, also at Halifax, was altered in 1862, these galleries were added to it. The same idea was also incorporated into the design of the two towers at Key West in Florida. Their purpose was for observation on the base of the tower and for firing downwards at the enemy in case of sapping or mining or any attempt to scale the walls.

With the conclusion of the war with France in 1783, it was decided to bring Guernsey's defences up to date by building fifteen small round towers in association with coastal batteries. The design was inferior to the ones on Jersey. The base diameter was only 20ft and the vertical stone walls were 4ft thick and frequently pierced by openings or *créneaux*. The chief interest of these towers lies in the report of the Committee of Royal Engineers sent to inspect them in the summer of 1787 when work on them was nearly completed. Their report dismissed them as almost useless. It pointed out that because of '. . . the smallness of their diameter, the fire from their *créneaux*, and even from their top, is very inconsiderable. . . For the security of batteries, we approve of towers, but would recommend a different construction.'[4] Bearing this last sentence in mind, it is significant that two of the officers of this three-man inspection team were members of the Committee of Royal Engineers called upon to advise on the sites and design for the South Coast towers in England in 1803. They were Lieutenant-Colonel Robert Morse, who became Inspector-General of Fortifications, and Lieutenant-Colonel Abraham D'Aubant, who in the interval between serving on these two committees was in Corsica at the time of the Mortella Point action. In view of the unsatisfactory report on the Guernsey towers, guns were never mounted on them and they were only used as barracks.

More interesting from the point of view of martello design, were fifteen round towers erected by the British in Minorca, to strengthen the existing system of watch-towers, when they occupied the island in 1798, and three small forts built in Guernsey in 1804. These buildings bear a marked resemblance in profile, section and dimensions and must have had an influence on the design of martellos, for they have the distinctive slope or batter to the walls, a solid central pillar and a domed roof supporting a flat gun platform surrounded by a parapet. The towers in Guernsey stand in the centre of a solid base which was used by the battery, an arrangement that foreshadows the later martellos at Key West. The Guernsey forts were built at L'Erée, Hommet and Rocquaine, and the dimensions of the tower at Rocquaine were:

height	26ft
base diameter	37ft
thickness of walls at base	5ft 6in[5]

The importance of the Minorca towers was that during this period of British occupation the island was used as a base for thousands of troops on their way to fight the French in Egypt. They were therefore well known to the army, among whom may have been numbered Captain W. H. Ford, the officer who proposed the used of towers as sea defences on the south coast of England. The Royal Engineer officer in charge of building the towers in Minorca was Captain Robert D'Arcy, and the commander of the island who was responsible for instigating them was Lieutenant-General Charles Stuart, who had been in Corsica during the British campaign.

Meanwhile, the first two towers to have a rightful claim to the name martello had already been built in South Africa. Purists—such as the late Commander Mead—may not be entirely convinced of this, but it would be splitting hairs to give the towers any other name. There is no doubt about their source of inspiration, for the man responsible for their building had been with the Mediterranean fleet off Corsica in 1794. Vice-Admiral George Elphinstone was Commander-in-Chief of the squadron sent in the following year to annex the Dutch colony at the Cape of Good Hope before it fell into French hands, and to establish a base to control the sea routes to India. Elphinstone became governor of the colony and when the British occupation was secured, he sailed on to India leaving Major-General James Craig behind as his deputy. As an attack was expected at any moment by either the French or Dutch fleet to recapture the colony, Craig's task was to strengthen its defences, particularly those of the Cape Peninsula, the narrow neck of land joining the Cape of Good Hope to the mainland. On one side of it is Cape Town and on the other Simon's Town. Two towers were begun in haste either in the very last weeks of 1795 or at the beginning of the next year, one in Cape Town and one in Simon's Town, and both were placed close behind batteries. The Cape Town tower, which became known as Craig's Tower, was part of the outer defences of the town, built in association with a battery at Salt River for protection against an attack along the coast from the north; it was demolished about a hundred years ago. But the Simon's Town tower still stands behind the South Battery in the East Dockyard and overlooking False Bay.[6]

The tower was built of rough stones and boulders, only the outer surface being dressed, and the walls were vertical. Its dimensions were:

height	25ft
base diameter	42ft
thickness of walls	6ft

There were two floors and a flat roof, and a 4ft square pillar passed through the centre of the building from the ground floor. A double doorway 20ft above ground level gave entrance to the first floor, the battery earthworks acting as a protection on the outside. On this floor the walls were pierced by three gunports which gave a clear field of fire over all approaches from the landward side. The roof had a parapet and two steps: one was a firing step for men with muskets and the other was probably to take the wheels of a traversing slide for a long gun. There is no evidence that guns were actually mounted, no doubt because the armed forces were short of guns when they left England—though this could have been quickly done had the need arisen.

Probably no detailed plan was made of the towers as they were built in an emergency, but two years after they were finished William Kirstermann, the Major commanding Royal Engineers at the Cape, made measured drawings of the one at Simon's Town in which it is described as a 'Block House.'[7] Some years later, in 1827, an official return of the Works of Defence at the Cape, gave a good description of the building in time of peace:

> A good work of its kind, two storeys high with Parapet and Platform at the top; commanding the entrance of the Bay and a Keep to the Battery. It is capable of containing 2 guns and Embrasures now converted into windows are carried through the walls.

A few months after the two Cape Colony towers were started, the foundation stone of the first tower to be built in North America was laid at Halifax in July 1796 with fitting ceremony by the Governor of Nova Scotia and the Commander-in-Chief, HRH Prince Edward, better known by his later title of the Duke of Kent and for the fact that he was father of Queen Victoria. Since his arrival to take up his appointment two years previously, he had been busy improving defence works in Halifax, a most important military and naval base in British North America. The building of the first tower in Halifax was prompted by the news of the arrival of a French fleet off the West Indies. In case it joined forces with a Dutch fleet already known to be in the same waters, and sailed up the American coast to attack the port, Prince Edward set about strengthening the existing fortifications. Although no such attack took place, two more towers were built during the same period which, while they were martellos is spirit, purpose and inspiration, did not really measure up to this classification in design or construction. They were, however, of great importance with regard to the development of the towers.

The three early Halifax towers were all designed by the Commanding Royal Engineer, Captain James Straton, and although each plan was different, they had much in common.[8] They were all large and able to accommodate between 100 and 200 men; they were built of local stone with roofs made up of layers of unseasoned timber, which proved later to be a great source of trouble and expense. Unlike the two Cape Colony towers, there was no strong central pillar to support the roof and act as a pivot for a traversing gun. Instead, the centre of the building was occupied by a hollow cylindrical shaft varying in size from 8 to 13ft. This was used for an ammunition hoist from the ground-floor magazine to the roof and, while it was an ingenious labour-saving device, it must have weakened the towers' construction. The towers were named by Prince Edward after his brothers.

The one begun in July 1796 was called the Prince of Wales Tower; in one way or another, it was a cause of trouble for many years. In his anxiety to start building, the prince omitted to get official consent from the Board of Ordnance for funds for the tower, and for this was reprimanded. Within a few years of the tower's completion large sums of money were constantly being paid out for its repair. It was built at Point Pleasant in front of the citadel, to command the passage of the North West Arm and provide effective cover for Fort Ogilvie and two batteries. It could accommodate 200 men, although it was never garrisoned, and in case of attack was to be manned by local volunteers, merchant sailors in port at the time and a few men from the Royal Artillery. Its dimensions were:

height	28ft
base diameter	71ft
thickness of walls at base	8ft
decreasing to	6ft at the crest

It had two storeys, the ground floor being the magazine. The main entrance was into the first floor, at high level, but there was another entrance door on the ground floor which may, however, have been added later. In the walls of the first floor were three gunports and 6-pounder guns to fire through them. A timber parapet pierced by a number of embrasures surrounded the wooden roof, on which two 24-pounder guns and four 68-pounder carronades were mounted. By 1809 the roof was so rotten that it could no longer support the weight of the carronades and they had to be removed. Major repairs were necessary in the next year and a proper masonry parapet and bomb-proof roof replaced the offending wooden constructions. This was on the advice of Brigadier-General William Twiss who, as will be seen in chapter 4, had by this time had plenty of experience in building martello towers. It was only after this work was finished that the Prince of Wales Tower could be said to come anywhere near being classed as a martello. Despite all its shortcomings, though, this tower is still standing.

The other two towers, the Duke of York's and the Duke of Clarence's, were begun in or just before 1798 and both were demolished except for the bottom storey before the end of the last century. The Duke of York's Tower was built on Sandwich Point opposite Point Pleasant; it was inside the wall of the York Redoubt, situated on high ground 190ft above sea level, where it was thought to be out of the range of enemy naval guns. The tower was placed to the rear of an eight-gun battery, with which it was connected by two radial lines of palisades. It had many of the same features as the first tower and appears to have been a smaller version of it. Its base diameter was between 40ft and 50ft and it had room for one hundred men, half the number that could be accommodated in the Prince of Wales Tower.

The Duke of Clarence's Tower, built in the centre of the fort of the same name, was the most complicated of all three towers and had several interesting features. It acted as the keep to the fort as well as the barracks and could house 164 men. It was the only one of the towers built with three storeys and a flat roof as well as a dry ditch or moat. The ditch was circular and 7ft wide with an 8ft vertical counterscarp and contained two caponiers, or works with loopholes for firing through, constructed in the base of the ditch to prevent an enemy becoming established. This means of defence was used in the Kingston martellos, built in Ontario fifty years later, but the caponiers were of a different design, the ones at this tower being in the form of covered passageways. The dimensions of the tower were:

height	42ft
base diameter	50ft
thickness of walls	6ft

The stage was now set for the final martello design to appear. The inspiration was there and much valuable experience had already been gained by the Royal Engineers. By the beginning of the nineteenth century there were round towers for coastal defence in a number of places. Of the pre-Mortella Point action period there were Conway's towers in Jersey and the inadequate ones in Guernsey. Of the post-Mortella Point period there were the towers built in Minorca and Guernsey, the pair of early martellos in South Africa and the three at Halifax, Nova Scotia. So far no design was entirely satisfactory. It now remained for the necessary impetus to be given so that a perfected plan could be drawn up, not for one or two towers only but for mass production, and not at local command level in some far corner of the empire but at headquarters, as a concerted effort by the best military architects and with the blessing of the Board of Ordnance. The stimulus for this enterprise was soon given by Napoleon's invasion plans. As it happened, two designs appeared in quick succession. One was for the towers in Ireland, which preceeded the English design by a matter of months. It was for a simple stone tower, lacking some of the characteristics and expert engineering devices of its English counterpart. When the plan for this finally appeared in the autumn of 1804, it was both skilful and ingenious. More towers were built to this design than any other and it became the standard by which all other martellos were judged.

Notes and references to this chapter are on page 163

CHAPTER FOUR

THE ENGLISH SOUTH COAST DEFENCES

With Napoleon building an invasion fleet on the other side of the Channel, Britain had to look closely at the state of her coastal defences. Her first line of defence being the sea, she regarded the coastline of the Continent of Europe as her ultimate boundary, and the policy of blockade as her chief defensive weapon. Her greatest danger was to have the fleet absent in an emergency, and with this in mind, and the Welsh and Irish raids fresh in people's memories, the government made plans to meet any full-scale invasion that might be attempted.

A landing by the Boulogne flotilla could be expected at almost any point along the coast of Kent or Sussex. Although the Channel is narrowest at Dover, where the straits are only 22 miles wide, it was thought that not even Napoleon would be arrogant enough to try to enter England by her traditional and well-guarded front door. However, there was ample opportunity of easy access on the sparsely populated flat coast to the west, contained between the two formidable natural hazards of the cliffs of Dover and Beachy Head. These two chalk headlands are the seaward ends of two ridges of hills, the North and South Downs, and the relatively flat land enclosed by them, known as the Weald, falls away to a series of marshes at the coast. The greatest area of marsh is the vast tract of Romney Marsh in Kent, bounded on the west by another natural obstacle, the shingle promontory of Dungeness. Beyond this headland and the river Rother at Rye, the marshes continue in Sussex at Pett Level and, after a break in the Hastings and Bexhill district of some twelve miles between Cliff End and Cooden where a ridge of hills comes down to the sea in low cliffs, are extended westwards almost to Beachy Head in Pevensey Level. These marshes or levels have for centuries been jealously guarded, carefully drained and controlled areas of rich pasture, their main ditches having sluice gates and outfalls into the sea. The shore itself on all the low-lying ground presented no landing problems, being rock free shallow water. Such a coastline was an open invitation to an invader and had, in fact, been the scene of both the Roman and Norman landings. Once ashore, the enemy had every chance of making good headway through the Weald towards London by way of the gaps in the North Downs.

A plan for this vulnerable area was drawn up, to be put into effect when the signal was given that the Boulogne flotilla had put to sea. It was based on the theory of 'denying the enemy', and consisted of removing anything that might be of use to them once a foothold had been gained. Today it is called 'the scorched earth' policy. The inhabitants of the coastal area were to be evacuated to prearranged inland gathering places, taking with them all their livestock and destroying any goods they were unable to carry, preferably by burning.[1] At the same time, the coastal marshes were to be flooded by opening the sluice gates and letting in the sea at high tide, and even by knocking a hole in the sea wall at Dymchurch. This would ensure that the thousands of animals that grazed there every summer were removed by their owners and would not fall into enemy hands, and the rising water would prove a hindrance to progress inland.

The army did not favour the evacuation plan because it interfered with their own arrangements. They intended holding troops inland to be moved to the coast at speed at the crucial moment, and they foresaw ugly scenes on the inadequate roads with loose animals and frightened people moving in the opposite direction to themselves. Eventually the plan was abandoned as impracticable, mainly because it was realised that there would be insufficient time for the evacuees to carry out their preparations before leaving home. However, the precaution of flooding the marshes was retained as the 'ultimate deterrent', although it was understood how unpopular it would be and that local opposition could be expected. When the martellos were built, their sites were planned in conjunction with this scheme, and towers were placed in pairs to defend the sluice gates.

After 1803 when war was renewed there was growing public demand for more protection and it was decided that the coasts themselves must be fortified as the only sure means of keeping out the French. Barracks and camps were established near the coast and existing batteries were strengthened and new ones built. The vulnerable part of the coast from Beachy Head to Dover was examined during the late summer of 1804 to select sites for the martello towers, and by this time six batteries were in existence. Two of them were in Sussex near Eastbourne; the West Battery was situated at Langney Point and the East Battery was to the east of it on the shingle waste called the Crumbles. In Kent there were three new batteries in the Hythe area, twelve miles west of Dover; this was considered the most likely place for the French to land, and there was an epidemic of military building here. The batteries were between the eastern end of Dymchurch Wall and Shorncliffe, and were called Moncrief, Sutherland and Twiss. This last was named after the Commanding Engineer of the Southern District, Brigadier-General William Twiss, an expert in defence works, who figured largely in the story of martello towers and was, as will be seen, the key figure in their story and the man responsible for their very existence.[2] The sixth battery was at Folkestone; it was described as the 'old Battery', and was considered to need troops to support it 'to prevent an enemy forcing his way through that Town, to the interior'.[3]

Monumental works had been going on for some time at Dover, too, finishing work that had been started during the American War of Independence and adding to the defence system which had accumulated from pre-Roman times. Not only was there accommodation for a mobile force of 5,000 to 6,000 men, capable of being rushed forward to any engagement, but for thousands more as well, as this fortress had been chosen as the last stronghold of the British army where the final stand against the enemy would be made.

All the steps taken so far to counter invasion were of a conventional nature, but two quite original ideas were put forward also. One of these was the Royal Military Canal, which met with no opposition and was hurried into being as soon as it was suggested in September 1804. It was not a canal to carry traffic, but a wet-ditch or moat some 30 miles long from Shorncliffe in Kent to the river Rother at Rye in Sussex. Its purpose was to act as a retrenchment to the natural bastion of Dungeness and to cut off and isolate the whole of the Romney Marsh area. Later the canal was extended from Rye to Cliff End near Hastings to cut off Pett Level in the same way. The canal, it was thought, might replace the drastic measure of flooding the marshes, a scheme that was in any case too slow in an emergency to be effective, as it would take more than one tide for the water to reach an appreciable level. The proposal for the canal came from a Lieutenant-Colonel John Brown and its construction was not carried out by the Board of Ordnance but was treated as a 'field work', a temporary fortification built in an emergency. The work was under the direction of the eminent civil engineer Sir John Rennie, using some skilled Royal Engineers labour but mainly civilian 'navigators' and labourers. It was a fine piece of engineering of a landscape nature. A military road was built on the landward side and there were picturesque gun turrets or station houses every quarter of a mile. It cost £200,000 ($480,000) but despite the expense its futility was apparently realised as soon as it was finished, for the guns were never mounted and in 1806 it was stocked with tench. It is hardly surprising that in his *Rural Rides* William Cobbett, the radical journalist and acute observer, made some caustic comments. 'Here is a canal . . . made for the length of thirty miles . . . *to keep out the French*; for those armies that had so often crossed the Rhine and the Danube, were to be kept back by a canal, made by Pitt, thirty feet wide at the most'.[4] When the sites for the martello towers were finally chosen, however, the canal was brought into the scheme and tower no 30 at Rye was built to defend the sluices at its western end and no 38 at Cliff End, the terminal of the Pett Level extension.

The second original idea was for 'Towers as Sea-Fortresses', which came to be known as martello towers; this was put forward a few weeks after hostilities were renewed in the summer of 1803, long before the Royal Military Canal was suggested. Unlike the canal, this project met with delays and difficulties of every kind. Although a great many senior officers conversant with towers as sea defences were stationed in Britain after the year-long peace, it was left to a young Royal Engineers officer, Captain W. H. Ford, to make the suggestion.[5] As mentioned in the previous chapter it is possible that he may have seen the ones in Minorca. However, the Mortella Point incident was so well known and had been so thoroughly discussed, especially by the Royal Engineers and the Royal Artillery, that Ford was undoubtedly well informed on the subject.

Ford's plan proposed a chain of towers along the Channel coast of Kent and Sussex, built at short intervals in order that their fire crossed at almost point-blank range.[6] The towers were to be square and to carry a gun on the flat roof that traversed a full circle, thus increasing the chance of hitting a moving ship at sea. Ford listed the chief merits of towers as sea-fortresses which eventually applied to all martellos wherever and whenever they were built. Their main advantage was that they would be so substantially built that they would be long-lasting and their maintenance would be negligible. In peacetime, the guns could be dismantled and stored inside the building and the tower closed up until another emergency arose—in modern terms, they could be 'mothballed', like battleships. As to manning the towers, only a small garrison would be needed and if an enemy landing took place, the towers were equipped to withstand a lengthy siege. They would also be quick and easy to build as well as cheap, and at a rough estimate Ford thought they would cost less than £3,000 ($7,200) each.

He sent his proposals to his superior officer, Brigadier-General Twiss. Impressed by the novel idea but not convinced by the full extent of the scheme, Twiss passed it on to the Master of Ordnance and to General Sir David Dundas, the officer who had captured the Mortella Point Tower in 1794.[7] Twiss added his own recommendations to the memorandum, which made it clear that in principle he approved of towers, but not on the scale that Ford had suggested. He recommended them only to support batteries, for the most obvious landing places and the marshland sluices. This was, in fact, the opinion given every time that Ford's plan was considered and became the principle adopted by the Committee of Royal Engineers when the coast was later surveyed for the tower sites.

Ford's plan then began its tedious journey to acceptance. It was fifteen months before it emerged with the seal of authority conferred upon it by Privy Councillors and the chief military officers responsible for coastal defence. In many respects it was altered, but it still contained the germ of his plan. On its way it stirred up controversy and opposition on all sides, and not a little acrimony and derision. Not only was the whole country divided on the subject of towers, but so was the army, and in Parliament it was a matter for questions and hot debate. It was probably the last occasion when a member of the royal family took sides in a major military issue. The Duke of York, as Commander-in-Chief, perhaps remembering the tower named after him at Halifax in Nova Scotia, urged that the towers be built at once as field-works, a course which was soon to be taken in Ireland. As to the navy, they were in favour of them and asked that they should be built. This was not surprising, as the commander of the fleet in home waters was Admiral Lord Keith, formerly Vice-Admiral George Elphinstone of the Cape of Good Hope expedition. More important still, the First Lord of the Admiralty was none other than Admiral Sir John Jervis, now Lord St Vincent, who had written so enthusiastically and with such foresight after the Mortella Point action that he 'hoped to see such works erected... on every part of the coast likely for an enemy to make a descent on'.

When Ford's proposals reached the Secretary of State for War, he asked that the Committee of Royal Engineers should examine the scheme and give their opinion on the technical side of the plan. Twiss was one of the members of the committee, and the other two were the engineer officers who sixteen years before had inspected the Guernsey round towers, Lieutenant-General Robert Morse, now Inspector-General of Fortifications, and Colonel Abraham D'Aubant. Their report concluded, as we have seen, that while they approved of towers for the support of smaller batteries, a different design was needed. No doubt because they were overworked, it was nine months before the committee even wrote a report, and this was after some pressure had been brought to bear by the cabinet summoning them to appear before them in April 1804. But still no design for the tower had been put forward. If Pitt had not been returned to power as prime minister at this time, there might have been further delay, but he was eager to press on with anti-invasion schemes and was known to be interested in the towers. This interest had probably

Page 53 (above) Tower at Petit Bot, Guernsey, one of a range of towers built on the island before the Mortella Point action but pronounced ineffective by the Royal Engineers; *(below)* Simon's Town, South Africa, one of the first two martello towers to be built in 1796, from a photograph taken in 1868

Page 54 (above) Martello tower on Dalkey Island, Dublin Bay, Ireland; this is tower 9 to the south of Dublin; *(below)* Joyce's Tower, Sandycove, Co Dublin, from an oil painting by Rigby Graham

been aroused by Colonel John Moore when he was stationed at Shorncliffe Camp, and Pitt was living at nearby Walmer Castle in the capacity of Lord Warden of the Cinque Ports. It was this same Colonel Moore who had been with the gunners when the Mortella Point tower was finally captured.

In the late summer of 1804 Twiss spent some time surveying '...all the Coast between Beachy Head in Sussex and Dover in Kent, distant by Road some 66 miles, but having a Coast of greater length...'[8] His aim was to examine the ground to see what more could be done to improve the defences, and where to site the towers. A letter written by him on 3 September, part of which is quoted below, to the Inspector-General of Fortifications, Lieutenant-General Robert Morse, embodied a masterly report on the terrain and a programme extending from 1804 to 1806, for building fifty-eight towers and throwing bomb-proof arches over some of the towers of the Tudor Sandgate Castle to 'render it a secure sea battery'. At the same time, he made it quite clear that, although towers were already going up in Ireland, still no design had been worked out for the South Coast towers.

> My first object was to apply the general Principles of Fortification, which the Committee of Royal Engineers had approved, for the Defence of this exposed Line of Coast, and it occurred tome [sic], that the simple Tower, of about 29 feet diameter, arched over, and having on its top, one heavy Gun, and two Carronades, would apply throughout, by placing them within five or six hundred yards of each other, in the most advantageous landing places, and extending their distances as Circumstances might render admissable.
>
> I communicated this Idea to the General Officers employed on this Coast, and I had the satisfaction to find... this System of Defence a decided preference, to any

Works of Greater Magnitude, which after incurring the same expense, must have larger Intervals.

The design for the towers had to be hurried forward by the military architects, for at this point the Privy Council decided, because of the widespread opposition to the project, to hold a conference on coastal defence as a whole at Rochester in Kent on 21 October. Exactly one month after Twiss wrote the letter quoted above, another was written to the Inspector-General of Fortifications, giving a brief and lucid description of a 'Bomb Proof Tower' before the final modifications were made. It was signed by Twiss, D'Aubant and a third engineer officer named Lieutenant-Colonel Thomas Nepean, who ten years previously had been a member of a reconnoitring party sent ashore before the action at Mortella Point.

> We beg leave to submit [the letter ran] the following description of a Project we have formed of a Bomb Proof Tower, for the defence of the coast, without waiting until the drawings of it are finished, which are now in hand. The interior circle of the tower has a diameter of 26 feet, and the area at the top is calculated to receive one 24 pounder Gun, and 2 Carronades of the same calibre, all mounted on traversing platforms, to fire over a high parapet, the crest of which is about 33 feet above the foundation. The ground floor to contain a powder magazine and cistern with room for provisions, fuel and other stores. The middle floor to lodge a garrison of one officer and 24 men, having an entrance placed 10 feet above the exterior ground. In this Project the centre Pillar is solid, and a stone staircase is contrived in the exterior wall which at that part is so encreased in thickness as to render it everywhere equally strong.

The Rochester conference adopted the bomb-proof tower

project with one dissenting voice; this was Lieutenant-Colonel John Brown, the perpetrator of the Royal Military Canal. The work was to be undertaken by the Board of Ordnance, and the towers were to be circular because they would be cheaper than the square ones Ford had proposed. There were to be three sorts of bomb-proof tower. The largest were really independent forts to house some 350 men and mount eleven guns, and were never known as martellos when the name became popular.[9] They were called redoubts or simply circular forts. One was planned for Seahouses to the east of Eastbourne and another at Rye Old Harbour. Later this was

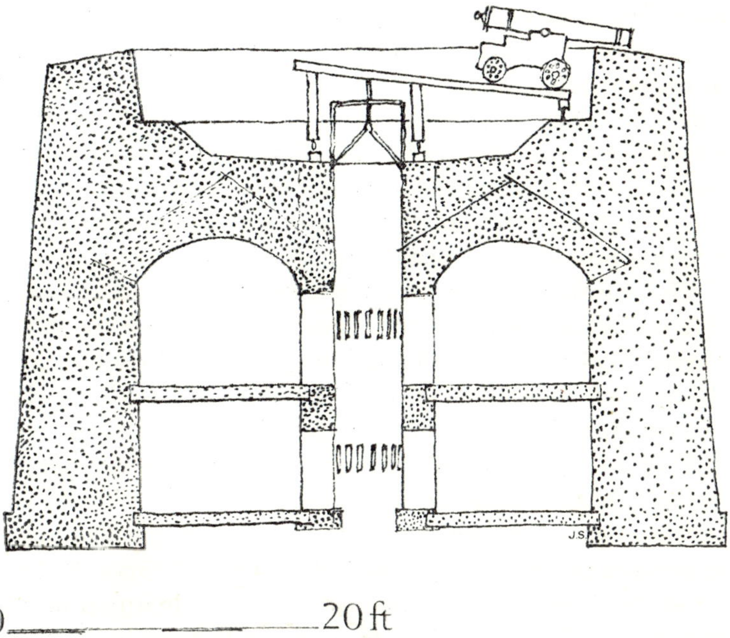

Section of a martello tower redrawn from an untitled sketch in the Public Record Office (WO/55/778). This was probably the original drawing produced for the Rochester conference on coastal defence in October 1804

changed and the Rye fort idea was dropped, but one of this class was built at the eastern end of Dymchurch sea wall. This took the place of the only one of the second class to be planned, namely a four-gun tower. As well as these, Sandgate Castle was to be altered as Twiss had proposed in his original survey. For the rest, eighty-three towers were proposed, all to conform to the description contained in the letter signed by Twiss, D'Aubant and Nepean quoted above. These were the towers which eventually bore the name martello. They were to be armed with one 18-pounder long gun and, by using Lieutenant-Colonel Nepean's 'ingenious contrivance', two carronades or short naval guns of the same calibre. Unfortunately this contrivance was not described and never materialised; probably it was a miniature traversing platform, similar to the one on the roof of the Mortella Point tower shown on page 35, as there was only room to accommodate the one long gun properly on the tower roof. Certainly, Twiss informed Morse five days after the conference that experiments were in progress on traversing platforms and Nepean's may have been one that proved to be unsuccessful.[10]

The number of towers that were to be built was changed several times. Within a few days of the conference it was altered to three towers of the largest class and eighty-one of the smallest as well as 'an enclosed Work on Anthony Hill, of a nature to be determined hereafter'.

By the late autumn of 1804 all that remained was for the building of the towers to begin but, in common with the rest of this long story of procrastination, and with Napoleon ready to pounce, this was also delayed. Poor Twiss, being called upon by the Board of Ordnance to give a weekly report on the progress of the towers, had to write on 9 November, 'I can only state, that they are not yet begun and from the lateness of the Season, and the few materials collected, my opinion is, that it will not be proper to begin them, until the Spring'.[11] At the same time, he was worried that a contractor had not been appointed, as he wrote to Morse on the same date:

> I am much concerned that the Honorable [sic] Board have not appointed some respectable and responsible Contractor, for erecting the proposed Towers, on the Coast, in the Southern District, and the more so as at present, I do not know, of any proper Person to contract and execute these Works.

During the winter months ahead, before the beginning of the new building season, a great deal of preparatory work had to be done. Besides finding a 'proper person' to undertake the work and materials to carry it out, land had to be acquired by the Board of Ordnance on which to build the towers. Negotiations were started and it appears that the board preferred to buy freeholds or lease the land rather than buying it outright. The land on which no 42 at Bulverhythe, for example, was built was leased for ninety-nine years at a rent of £7 per annum. The amount of land required varied, but each tower was usually surrounded by a sizeable patch which sometimes contained subsidiary domestic buildings or the battery it supported. Tower E, for example, at Clacton stood in a patch measuring almost four acres.

At last, in the spring of 1805, the building of the South Coast towers began, nearly two years after Ford had first suggested them. The line of towers planned had been extended in Sussex from Seahouses almost to Beachy Head at Eastbourne. By the end of the summer, when Napoleon's Army of England faced about and headed at full speed for Austria, England's Channel coast was a shambles of partly-built forts, barracks and martello towers. Although in October Trafalgar was fought and won and Britannia ruled the waves, the towers continued to be built. By the end of the next summer, 1806, only six of the towers were finished and it was two more years before they were all completed. When the work was finished in 1808, there were two eleven-gun towers or circular forts and seventy-three of the one-gun towers or martellos. Despite the fact that the threat of invasion was over, the idea of martellos had come to stay. As soon as the ones on the south coast were finished, the East Coast towers were started. Twenty-nine martellos were built here and at the same time one more was added to the South Coast towers at Seaford in Sussex. By 1812, when all the English towers were finished, a comprehensive and unique defence system of 103 martello towers had been established and not one of them fired a shot in anger.

Notes and references to this chapter appear on pages 164-5

CHAPTER FIVE

THE PLAN AND CONSTRUCTION OF THE ENGLISH MARTELLO TOWERS

Following the long drawn out deliberations, the towers at last went up along the coasts of England between 1805 and 1812. The original project for the South Coast towers was scarcely completed before a second range on the east coast was begun. These had been proposed as early as October 1805 but it was not until 1808 that plans for them were put in hand and building began in the following year. They stretched from near Clacton in Essex at the mouth of the Thames estuary to Aldeburgh in Suffolk, guarding some of the loneliest river mouths and marshes in the country. Both groups of towers conformed in most respects to the original design described in the letter to the Inspector-General of Fortifications dated 4 October 1804 and quoted on page 56, but it was the South Coast towers that followed the plan almost exactly, with some modifications and improvements added before building started. This design was of great importance because it was taken as the standard for all later martello towers.

The two groups of towers had more features in common than differences. Briefly, they were small, round, built of brick covered with a cement and sand stucco, some 33ft in height from the ground level to the crest of the slightly projecting parapet with a single entrance doorway 20ft above the ground instead of the 10ft stated in the original description (see page 56). Inside was an unlit ground floor which was the magazine and store while the first floor was the garrison's quarters from which a stone staircase within the walls led to the flat roof or gun platform. Both groups had the characteristic 'upturned flower-pot' profile; this slight slope or batter was achieved by decreasing the thickness of the external walls from the base of the building to the top by some 6ft to 8ft. In some of the East Coast towers this slope was greatly exaggerated on the seaward side. The main differences between the two groups were in shape and size. Although at first sight both may appear to be round, the South Coast towers were slightly elliptical while the East Coast towers were ovoid or even cam shaped. The towers on the east coast were larger, enabling them to have two staircases instead of one, four windows instead of two and to accommodate more armament on the roof and more men in the living quarters.

In true military style, the South Coast towers were numbered for identification purposes. Usually a small stucco tablet with Roman numerals incised into it was let into the wall above the entrance door, but no 23 at Dymchurch had a thin slate tablet instead. No 24, however, had painted Arabic figures, though there is no guarantee that this was the original marking. For variety in this sequence, no 25 appears not to have displayed a number at all, although if it had been painted on it could easily have disappeared over the years. The towers were numbered from east to west, starting with no 1 above East Wear Bay to the east of Folkestone and ending with no 73 near Beachy Head at Eastbourne, a martello better known as the Wish Tower. A seventy-fourth tower was added to this range in 1810, two years after the others were finished. This was at Seaford, some twelve miles west of the Wish Tower, at the end of the natural defences of the great chalk cliffs of Beachy Head and the Seven Sisters.

The East Coast towers were recognised by the letters of the alphabet, starting with A at St Osyth in Essex and working northwards. As there were twenty-nine towers, the last three were known as AA, BB and CC. This group of towers had an odd man out—the last tower of all, at Slaghden just outside Aldeburgh in Suffolk, some ten miles beyond BB. It was completely different in design from any other martello, being quatrefoil in shape. The source of its design is difficult to establish. Perhaps it was inspired by one of the castles built on the south coast by Henry VIII; of these, it resembles Walmer Castle in Kent most closely. Alternatively, it could have been the design for the four-gun tower proposed in 1804 for the east end of Dymchurch Wall but never built. Finally, it is possible that its shape was influenced by the layout of the positions for guns on the roof of the East Coast towers.

It may therefore be said that, while there were in all 103 martello towers, seventy-four were built to the original design, twenty-eight to the later East Coast tower design and one was a complete outsider! Within the two groups of towers is a subdivision, namely those built with a dry ditch or moat. This extra protection was provided against the risk of the enemy, having come ashore, storming the building from the land. The idea was that the moat would act as a trap for enemy troops who, having let themselves down into it by ropes or ladders, could be picked off by musket fire from the tower roof before they attempted to scale the smooth stucco walls. The choice of towers equipped with them seems to have been arbitrary. They should have been constructed around towers in particularly exposed or vulnerable positions but in some cases it seems that they were selected by the luck of the draw. But at this distance of time it is not possible to judge accurately, since coastal erosion has changed the scene drastically in many places, and batteries and other defences have disappeared without trace. In general it was the cliff-top towers that were moated. However, the first three towers, built on the cliffs overlooking East Wear Bay in Kent, were an exception to this rule so that it appears that moats were not thought of until the building programme was actually started. There is certainly no mention of them in Twiss's letters and surveys of 1804. Some low-level towers were also moated, for example Seaford in Sussex and Aldeburgh in Suffolk. These two stood alone and were therefore known to be in a weak position; moats were not constructed where towers were built in long lines, as at Pevensey Bay, when they were at their strongest. Because of the number of towers that have disappeared over the years, it is difficult to make a complete record of the moated ones, but twelve have been identified among the South Coast towers and nine along the east coast.

A more detailed examination of the towers shows that the massive walls were the main feature of the building. In designing them, the guiding principle was to concentrate the greatest strength on the seaward or enemy side of the tower. For this reason the door and deeply recessed windows faced inland so that the building presented an unbroken wall surface to the sea. This was more successfully achieved in the South Coast towers, where the two windows were placed at 90° on either side of the door, leaving 180° of wall without any openings. In the East Coast towers, the unbroken wall was greatly reduced because the two pairs of windows on either side of the door were placed at 60° intervals, leaving only 120° of unbroken wall surface. Two ingenious pieces of construction were incorporated into the building. First, the towers were not true circles but, as we have already seen, elliptical or ovoid. In both cases, the shorter axis was placed parallel with the coast and thus the narrower part of the tower was on the sea side. Secondly, in order to have a denser mass of masonry in this vital area, the inner and outer circles of the tower walls were struck eccentrically. The thickness of the walls therefore tapered gradually from approximately 13ft at the base on the seaward side to 6ft at the sides and 5ft facing inland. The following measurements of the axes of the South Coast towers demonstrate the two features of the external walls, namely the elliptical shape of the tower and the slope or batter of the walls:

axes at the base of the tower	48ft and 45ft
axes at first floor level	45ft and 42ft
axes at roof top level	40ft and 37ft [1]

By way of comparison, the axes at the base of the East Coast towers were usually 55ft and 48ft.[2] It should be noticed that within both groups all measurements can vary slightly, a fact which has led to confusion and dispute. The variations are probably due to the different builders employed.

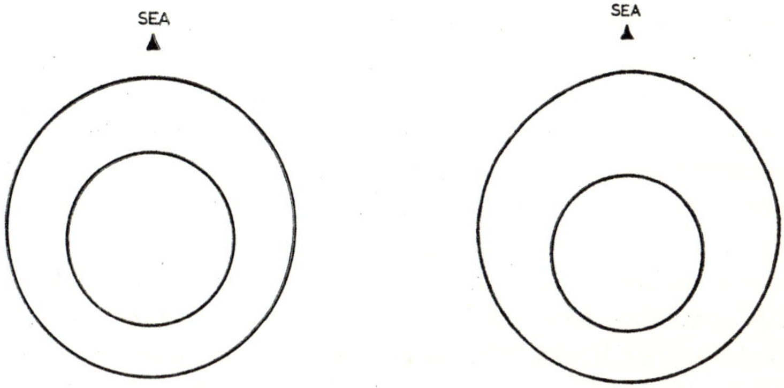

Diagrams demonstrating the ground level shape of: (left) a south coast tower; (right) an east coast tower

The strength of the walls was terrific. Experiments were carried out at Woolwich by the Royal Engineers before construction began to discover the strongest possible material both for bonding the bricks and for the exterior stucco coating. Cannonballs were fired at the walls to be tested until eventually the necessary strength was achieved and it was found that they bounced off the walls. The bricks were set in a mixture of lime, ash and hot tallow, known as hot lime mortar, which set as hard as iron. Mr Ronald Ward, the architect, who owns and has converted tower no 13 at Hythe in Kent, in a monograph he wrote on the tower, demonstrated the outstanding strength of this jointing material and the consequent solidity of the walls when describing the difficulties encountered by workmen engaged on the conversion. 'To remove any portion [of the walls] needs drills...' he wrote '...for one can only cut out sections in small pieces. It took two men with a compressor and two guns three weeks to form the wardrobe in our bedroom, size 7ft × 7ft × 3ft!' The previous owner of the tower, a builder named Glock, had experienced similar trouble, the mortar making it impossible for him to recover bricks needed to build partitions, and the exercise put up the cost of his work to such an extent that the alterations he was carrying out became unprofitable. Others who have demolished whole towers could testify to the strength of the walls. When no 22 at Dymchurch was destroyed by Kent County Council in 1956, it was more than all the modern equipment could deal with, and in the end explosives had to be used. Similarly, in 1860, when new types of heavy guns were tested on some of the martellos at grand Royal Artillery field days, they were hard put to it to make an impression on the buildings. It took fifty rounds each from a 100-pounder, an 80-pounder and a 40-pounder of the new rifled Armstrong guns to demolish no 68 on St Anthony's Hill near Eastbourne. And yet the sea can wash away a martello in huge chunks of masonry, with the bricks all firmly stuck together by mortar.

Built into the thickness of the walls were the staircases and the flues for the chimneys and for ventilation, all of them having their outlets in the parapet at the top of the tower. Mr Ward, in his monograph, commented in glowing terms on the construction of all three of these features in his own martello. Of the ventilating flues, which started on the ground floor and went up through the full height of the tower, he remarked that they were 'a really scientific job...arched beautifully in the thickness of the wall.' They were 1ft 3in wide and 1ft 6in high at the springing of the arch and wound round skilfully following the line of the tower perfectly. The chimney flues and stairways began at the first floor level. In the South Coast towers, a single stairway of twenty-five stone steps was built in the thickest part of the wall and emerged on to the roof by a door which had its back to the sea. The two stairways of the East Coast towers, however, started on the opposite side of the tower on either side of the entrance door and thus reached the roof in a dangerous position facing the sea and in full view of the enemy.

The flat roof, which was the tower's gun platform, was covered with lead and surrounded by a solid parapet usually 6ft high and at least 6ft thick. The roof space inside the parapet on the South Coast towers was circular, but on the

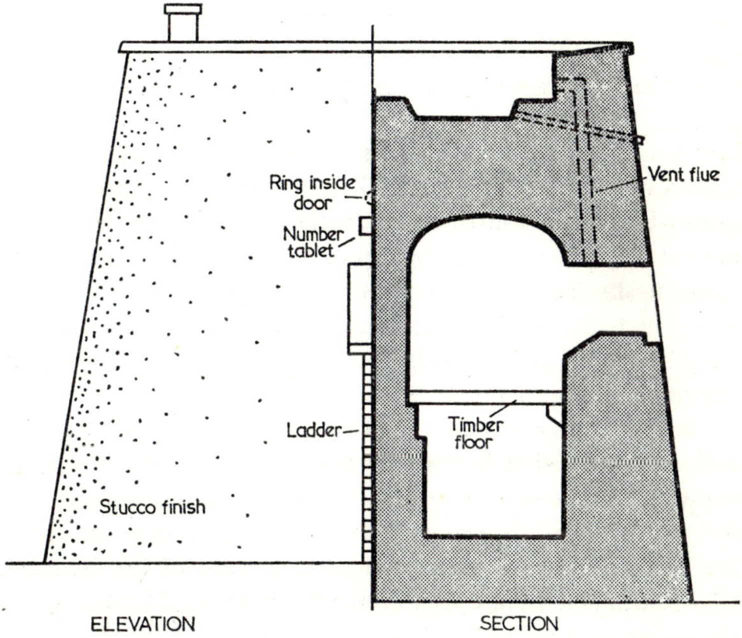

Elevation and section of tower no 13 at Hythe, Kent

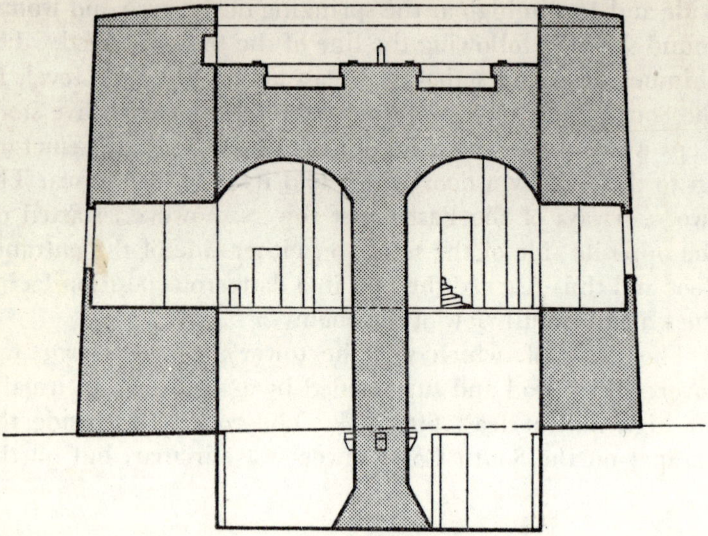

Section through tower no 23 at Dymchurch, Kent

East Coast towers it was shaped like a four-leafed clover, with the arcs of the circles nearest the sea and at the sides for the guns while in the fourth arc on the land side the two staircases appeared (see page 90). On top of the parapet were the conspicuous and incongruous chimneys. If the call for action had ever been given, these domestic details would presumably have been knocked off as they would have been in the path of the traversing gun.

Moving from one extreme of the building to the other, the foundations, which had a tremendous weight of masonry to support, went down to an unspecified depth and were arched for greater strength. From these foundations rose a fine circular brick pillar, the main structural feature of the interior, which supported not only the handsome vaulted roof but also the heavy gun above it; this rotated on a steel pivot sunk in its centre. The pillar was 5ft in diameter from the ground

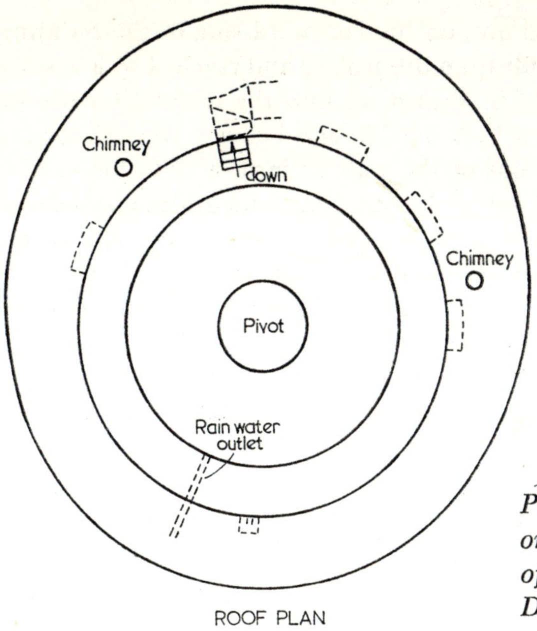

Plan of the roof or gun platform of tower no 23 at Dymchurch

floor to the first floor level, where it was cut back to take a wall plate to support the flooring joists and continued upwards to the roof. From the top of the pillar was sprung the arch of the roof which was an annular dome in the form of very thick vaulted brickwork. In his monograph, Mr Ward demonstrates how much the construction of the roof impressed him:

> These were groined arches, magnificently designed and executed, and the centering for this work would have puzzled some of our present day mechanics, for it is beautifully done, and above the arches there is a dense mass of brickwork up to 10ft in thickness from the crown up to the top of the building.

The characteristic single high-level entrance door was, as

has been pointed out, on the landward side of the building, approximately 20ft from the ground and reached by a wooden ladder that could be drawn up into the tower after use for security. The door was wooden and beneath the sill of some a space was cut out of the wall to form a slide for moving materials in and out of the building; such slides may be seen in no 23 and no 24 at Dymchurch (pages 72 and 89). In the case of moated towers, the drawbridge was the only means of access; it was hung from chains and a mechanism was provided for raising and lowering it.

The interior of the tower was divided into two floors; the high-level entrance door opened into the first floor which was the living quarters. A trap-door, which was usually to the left of the entrance, gave access to the ground floor by means of a ladder. A large iron ring was fixed into the roof immediately above the trapdoor; from this a block and tackle would have been suspended for hoisting stores and equipment into and out of the tower and up and down from the ground floor. The ground floor was reserved for the powder magazine and stores. In some towers, for example at Dymchurch, the floor space was divided into thirds by walls radiating from the central pillar. The first part, into which the

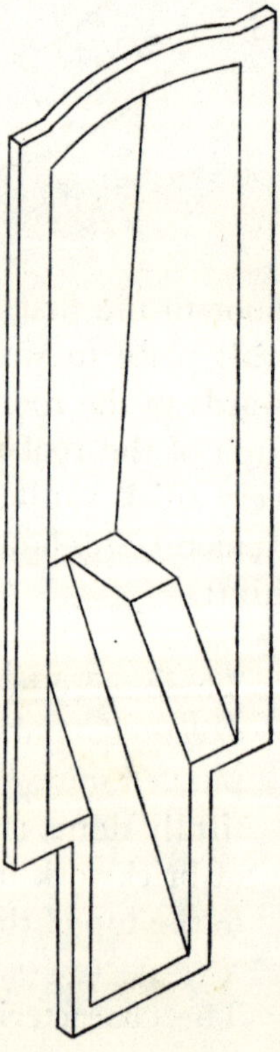

Isometric view of the entrance door at tower no 23 at Dymchurch, showing the slide beneath

Page 71 A view of the Thames East-Indiaman as she lay stranded near Eastbourne in February 1822. This engraving shows martello towers in close formation near Langney Point; they are nos 71, 70, 69, 68 and 67

Page 72 (above) View of Pevensey Bay by Alfred Clint (1807-1883); *(below)* martello tower no 23 at Dymchurch, Kent, awaiting restoration

ladder descended, was for stores, the part nearest the sea where the walls were strongest was the powder magazine and the other section was for the ammunition. Another arrangement, as at no 13 at Hythe, was to wall off about a third of the floor space on the seaward side for the magazine and ammunition, a larger space being left for stores. Some towers had a cavity hollowed out in the thickest part of the wall, presumably to hold the most dangerous material. A lighter box, similar to those in use in men-of war of the same period, was also kept in the magazine.

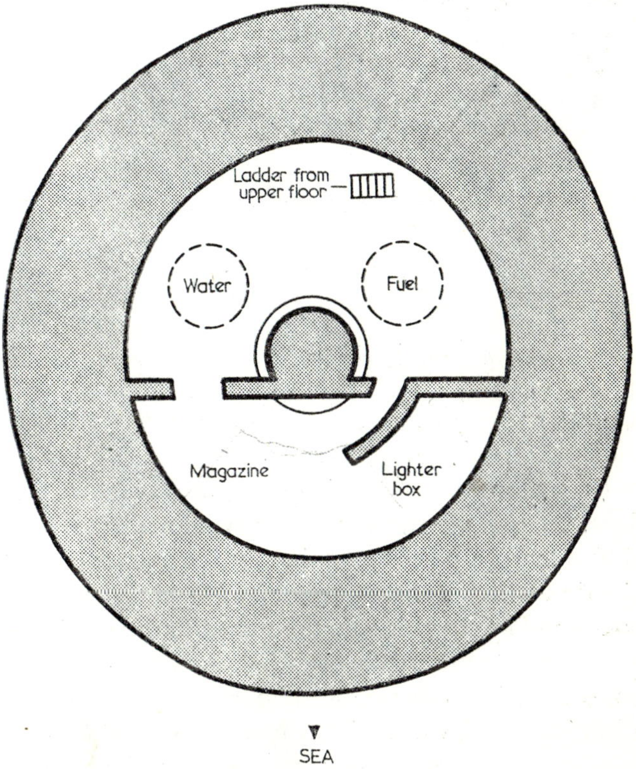

Ground floor plan of tower no 13 at Hythe

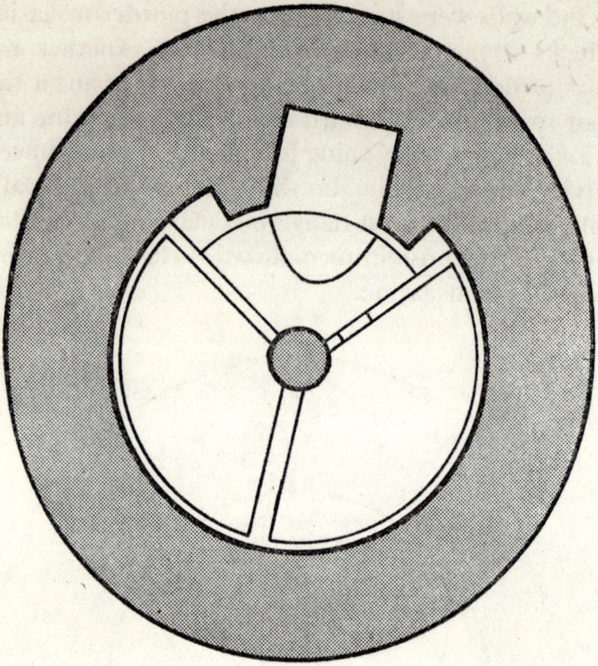

Ground floor plan of tower no 23 at Dymchurch, showing cavity in thickest part of the wall for highly inflammable materials

On the ground floor every precaution was taken to avoid accidents by fire. As there were no windows, light was provided by a lantern placed on a shelf in the magazine partition wall behind which a sheet of glass was fixed thus forming an internal window. In this way the naked flame was kept well away from the combustible material. As little metal as possible was used in constructing the magazine to avoid sparks; wherever metal was essential, copper was used as it is less liable to spark than other metals. The door hinges and latch were made of this material and the door itself was covered with a sheet of copper; on this was painted a list of the magazine's contents. Such a door still exists at martello no 5 at Folkestone.

As the tower was designed to withstand a siege, a large space was needed for stores. There was a container for fuel and a large water cistern, usually made of slate. Rain-water from the roof was not piped to this tank, as had been done in the Mortella Point tower, and the supply must have been brought in from outside. Some towers had wells sunk in the foundations where this was possible; others show signs of having had cellars below this level, perhaps for storing fuses and similar materials. It was no doubt these cellars that gave

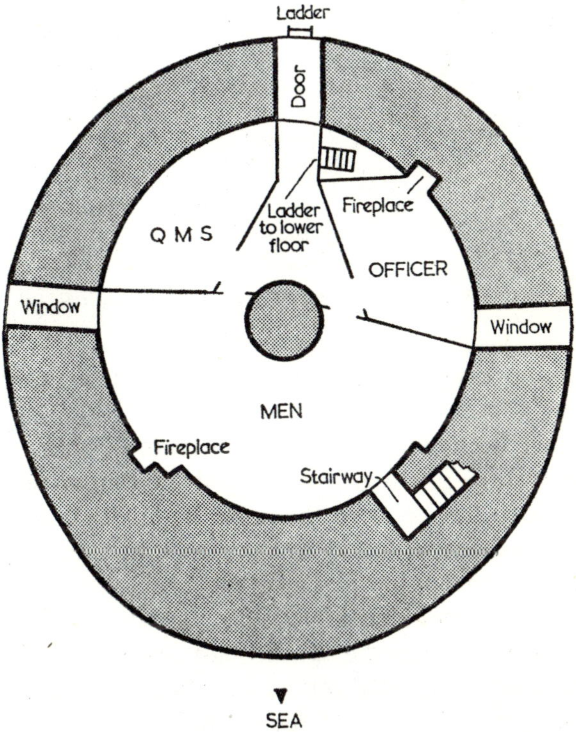

First floor plan of tower no 13 at Hythe

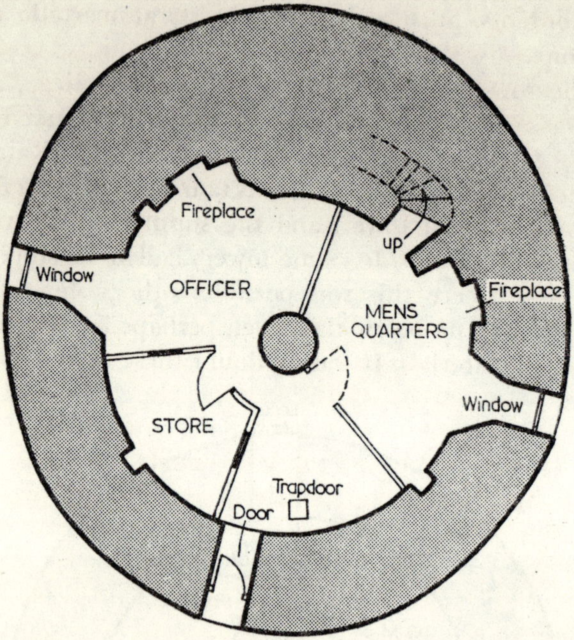

First floor plan of tower no 23 at Dymchurch

rise to the myths that still survive that some towers were connected by subterranean passages.

The first floor consisted of the garrison's living quarters; there were three rooms grouped round the central pillar with wooden partitions between them. Rather more than half the floor space was occupied by the quarters for the twenty-four men. It had one window and a fireplace and was intended for cooking, eating and sleeping. It was placed opposite the entrance doorway and in the South Coast towers the staircase to the gun platform opened out of it. There were usually two doors, one on either side of the central pillar, round which an arms stand was built to hold twenty-seven muskets. Of the two smaller rooms, one was for the officer and had a window and a fireplace, while a slightly smaller one which had no window was the quarter master sergeant's store. The disposition of these rooms varied; in some towers the officer's room was to the left of the entrance immediately beyond the trap-door and the store room was opposite, while in others, as at Dymchurch, the trap-door is to the right of the entrance and the storeroom to the left, followed by the officer's room and finally the men's quarters.

The floor boards, joists and wall plates were all of oak. The joists and 1¼in boards radiated from the wall plate round the pillar to a corresponding plate supported by stone corbels let into the inner surface of the exterior wall. Tower no 7 on Shorncliffe Heights in Kent has a floor laid in this way. Not many have survived because lack of ventilation led to dry rot in many towers and the remedy of scraping the woodwork and treating it with quick lime was ineffective.

As to the vital matter of the armament mounted on the roof, the original amount of one 18-pounder long gun and two carronades of the same calibre planned for the South Coast towers could not be accommodated, because apparently Nepean's 'ingenious contrivance' to take the carronades did not come up to expectations. Only a 24-pounder long gun was mounted, but the larger East Coast towers added smaller guns according to their position and needs; some had two carronades, some 5½in howitzers and some one of each. The gun was mounted on an oak carriage and revolved on a frame known as a slide which was attached to the pivot sunk into the centre of the roof over the brick pillar (see figure, page 57); on this it could traverse a full circle, a scale of degrees being marked on the inside of the parapet. The slide had an inclination of 1 in 12 and moved on wheels and metal tracks. A small track carried the wheels at the pivot end of the frame and beneath the parapet another track was fixed to a masonry course for the two wheels at the front of the slide to move on. The gun was hauled into position for firing by block and tackle; it was claimed that it could be worked by two men only entirely protected by the parapet. In the parapet were ammunition recesses for storing cannonballs; they were built with a small guard or fender in front to prevent the cannonballs rolling out. All the ammunition was passed up the stairs by hand from the ground floor magazine. This would have been more quickly accomplished in the East Coast towers with two staircases. A hole was cut in the door at the head of the stairs to pass the cartridge through to the gunners; the hole was fitted with a slide or small hinged door to cover it as a safety precaution in case of 'flash back' at the time of firing.

The amount of ammunition with which the towers were issued varied, of course, with the type of guns mounted. The East Coast towers usually had the following: [3]

100 round shot for the 24-pounder gun
20 case and grape shot for the same guns
40 case for the howitzers
280 various types of shell
40 howitzer carcases
80 hand grenades
380 flannel cartridges
120 bursters
½ ton of powder
1lb of slow match

Finally, the moats, where they occurred, were built of brick or dressed stone; they were some 40ft wide and 15ft or 20ft deep. The steep scarp, or glacis, formed the footing of the tower and had a batter of 3ft at the top; the counterscarp, or outer wall of the moat, was equally steep. It was formed not by digging down, but by piling soil against the counterscarp to form a ramp. This method of construction can be seen at Rye Harbour martello, no 28, where some of the soil of the ramp has disappeared and the brick buttresses built to strengthen the counterscarp are visible; it is also clearly seen on the seaward side of tower no 74 at Seaford. The tower door was reached by a drawbridge which, when drawn up, gave it extra protection. The doorcases of the moated East Coast towers are handsome, with the quoined dressed stone left unstuccoed and a heavy stone doorhead to take the drawbridge rings to which the chains were attached. The whole composition is reminiscent of the style of the eminent architect Carr of York.

Two moats had their own special defence features. This was a subsidiary trench, called a cunette, which was constructed at the foot of the tower and was filled with water. Tower no 30, in an important position near Rye where it guarded the sluices of the Royal Military Canal and two rivers, had one of these and so did tower N at Walton Ferry in Suffolk. Here the cunette was large, 20ft in width, and the dry moat itself was enormous, being 70ft wide.

A vast quantity of raw materials was needed for this project, by far the largest being the bricks. It was estimated that half a million were used in each South Coast tower, which Mr Ward reckons would build thirty four-bedroomed houses today; over 700,000 were needed for each East Coast tower. Local brick supplies were quite inadequate to deal with such demands and large quantities came from London brickworks. On the day that Morse, the Inspector-General of Fortifications, received Twiss's survey of the south coast for tower sites and his suggestion for 'the simple Tower of about 29 feet diameter' quoted on page 55, some bricks were ordered, apparently not without some trepidation. This was before the plans of the tower had been drawn, let alone approved, for the letter that makes this clear is dated 4 September 1804 and was written by Morse to the Board of Ordnance.[4]

Enclosed I send you copies of two letters from Brigr. General Twiss, received by this day's post, in conse-

> quence of which, and of your two private letters of the 31st August, expressing that Lord Chatham and Mr. Pitt approved of my suggestion of providing Bricks and workmen here, and of doing the work by contract, I have taken upon myself to authorize Mr. Adam to engage as many as two Millions of Bricks, and a number of Bricklayers, and to proceed in forwarding Bricks to the places mentioned in Brigr. Genl. Twiss's letter, without delay.
>
> This I have done under the strong impression that all possible dispatch was required. I have therefore to request that you will communicate the same to Lord Chatham, as soon as possible, that if his Lordship should not approve, I may stop in time.[5]

Mr Adam, mentioned in the letter, was a member of the firm of Adam & Robertson, builders' merchants, of 27 Old Bond Street. In order to allay suspicion and keep the price down, this firm placed their order with brickmakers scattered all over the London area, to be delivered to Tower Wharf for shipment to the south coast. However, London bricks were not used exclusively. This is obvious when the stucco has fallen off and the brickwork is exposed; the local bricks on the south coast are red in colour while the London ones are yellowish grey. There were many brickfields in the Wealden Clay belt of Kent and Sussex that stepped up their production as soon as the demand became known. The towers in the Bexhill area, for example, were built of brick brought by barge from Rye. Many of the bricks for the East Coast towers were made locally. In June 1808 the following report appeared in the press: 'The coasts of Essex and Suffolk are to be lined with Martello Towers in the same way as that of Kent. 500 men are now employed at Grays, in Essex, making bricks for the purpose.'[6]

Transporting the materials for this project was a mammoth undertaking. Rivers and canals were used wherever possible, as well as the sea, though this could be hazardous in time of war. Small boats and barges were loaded and beached as close as possible to the tower sites. For cliff top towers, however, the poor and inadequate roads were the usual means of access.

The building of the towers was carried out under the supervision of the Royal Engineers. As late as 9 November 1804 Twiss wrote to Morse, in the letter quoted on page 59, that no contractor had been appointed by the Board of Ordnance and he was despondent about finding a 'proper Person'. Such a person was later found in a Mr Hobson and he sub-contracted out to other builders, whose skill and ability varied. Generally the workmanship was of a high order, as Mr Ward points out in his monograph on tower no 13, but there were exceptions. At Dymchurch, for example, one of the towers had an outer skin of brickwork which was not bonded to the masonry beneath. The quality of work on the East Coast towers was usually higher than on the earlier ones, largely because by that time much experience had been gained in this type of building and, as there was no immediate threat of invasion then, the work was not so hurried. Claims have been made that the builders amassed great wealth from the project. The builder of the towers between Bexhill and Eastbourne, John Smith, was said to have made £20,000 ($48,000) profit and the descendants of another builder, Edward Hodges, say he made a fortune from martello towers.[7]

The cost of the towers was undoubtedly enormous. Ford originally estimated that each of the square towers he suggested would cost less than £3,000 ($7,200) and Twiss calculated £2,000 ($4,800) a tower for the cheaper round ones. The final figure must have been much larger as the cost of materials and freight rose, not to mention labour, for the project was not without strikes for pay increases. Whatever the cost, the work had to be paid for, and in May 1808 Twiss was ordered to measure the masonry contained in the towers so that Mr Hobson's annual account could be settled. Accordingly, Captain Cunningham and Captain Goldfinch, both of the Royal Engineers, were sent round Kent and Sussex respectively to measure up the work already done. Twiss wrote to the Board of Ordnance on the 29 May reporting that owing to uncompleted work and certain anomalies, he recommended the account be paid for the seventy-three towers only but that the forts or redoubts at Seahouses near Eastbourne and Dymchurch should be left unpaid for until all the work was completed.[8]

Britain paid dearly for the boost to morale that the martello project gave her. There had been criticism enough about the cost, let alone the necessity for them, during hostilities; when the clouds of war finally cleared, many people realised that they had been left with some extremely expensive white elephants. Perhaps the last word on the subject of cost should come from William Cobbett, written when he travelled through Kent in 1823:

> Here has been the squandering! Here has been the pauper-making!... To think that I should be destined to behold these monuments of Pitt...! Here they are, piles of bricks in a circular form... Cannons were to be fired from the top of these things, in order to defend the country from the French Jacobins! I think I counted along here upwards of thirty of these ridiculous things, which I daresay cost five, perhaps ten, thousand pounds each... I daresay they cost millions.

Notes and references to this chapter will be found on page 165.

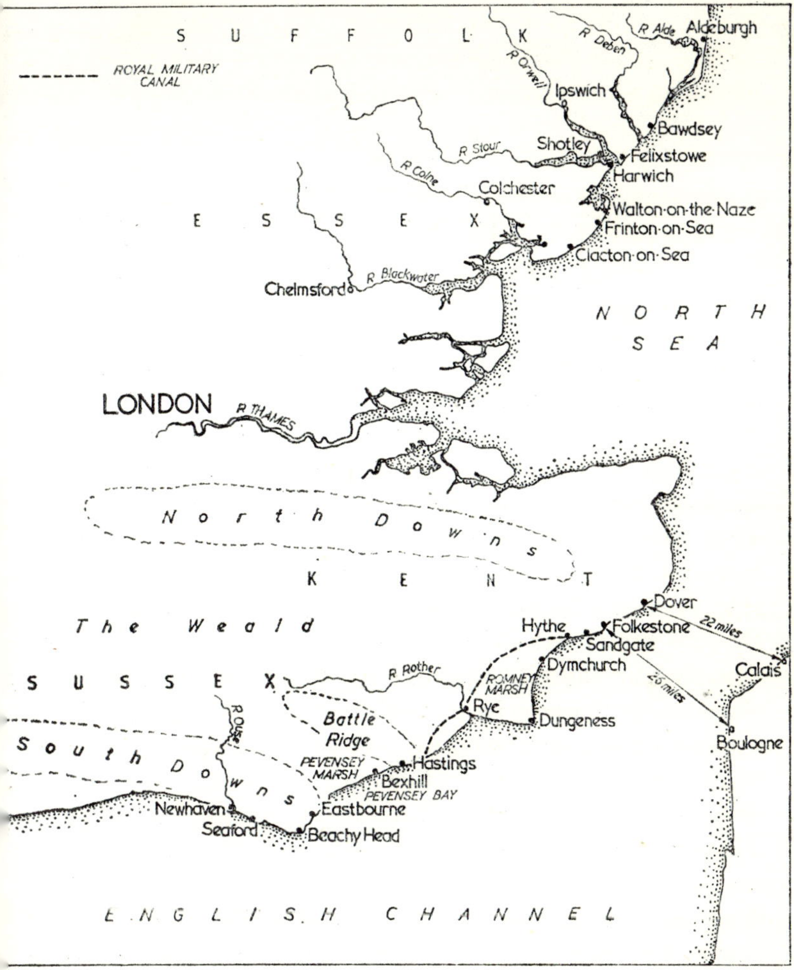

The English martello coastline—Sussex, Kent, Essex and Suffolk

CHAPTER SIX

DISTRIBUTION OF THE SOUTH COAST TOWERS

The distribution of the towers was dictated by geographical features and existing or planned defence works. In siting them, Twiss adhered to the general principles adopted by the committee of Royal Engineers which coincided with his own opinions put forward after first reading Ford's proposals. They were to be built, it will be remembered, to strengthen batteries, to protect any part of the coast particularly vulnerable to enemy landings and to guard the marshland sluices. By 1808 the towers stretched along the coast on cliff top and shoreline, arranged like beads on a too long string. They were placed singly in association with batteries and other military works, in pairs for mutual support on either side of the sluice gates and in long lines on low-lying coasts at approximately 600yd intervals so that the fire from their guns would cross. This last arrangement would have been by far the most effective had the towers ever been put to the test, as any defects they had disappeared in this formation. They were at their best at Pevensey Bay where a ship could be within range of fifteen towers. This was how Ford had envisaged them and today it is the only place on the south coast where the remaining low-level towers can be seen in anything like their original setting. Towers built on high ground have naturally survived better than those built at or near sea level, many of which have been swept away by the sea. Of the seventy-four built on the south coast—a total that includes the one added at Seaford—only twenty-six are still standing. Sixteen of the twenty-seven built in Kent have survived, while in Sussex there are only ten of the forty-seven left, because many of them were low-level towers.

KENT

The towers start to the east of Folkestone on the cliffs overlooking East Wear Bay, considered by Twiss to be a 'good landing', and continue to the end of the Romney Marsh coastline where the promontory of Dungeness projects into the sea. Here the deep, loose shingle was considered sufficient obstacle to the invader plus the fact that inundations would have taken place in Romney Marsh and to the west towards Rye. The positioning of the towers falls conveniently into three groups. First there was the cliff top group, nos 1 to 9, from East Wear Bay to the end of Shorncliffe Heights, a military camp then as now. This group of high-level towers, all of which are still standing, is subdivided into two sections. The first division consists of nos 1 to 3 overlooking East Wear Bay on one side and Folkestone harbour on the other; unlike other towers on high ground, these three are not moated, probably because this form of protection had not been thought of when building began. The second division in this group started on the west side of Folkestone town and these six all have moats or dry ditches. Next came a line of low-level towers, nos 10 to 21. They were almost equally spaced at the recommended 600yd intervals in front of Hythe, already a mass of new barracks, blockhouses and batteries as well as the commencement of the first stage of the new Royal Military Canal at Shorncliffe, to the point where Dymchurch Redoubt was built at the start of the sea wall. The third group consisted of three separate pairs of towers, nos 22 to 27, guarding the Romney Marsh sluice gates.

(*denotes that the tower is still standing)

Tower no

*1 The first tower was on the 200ft high cliff above East Wear Bay. Twiss proposed that the escarps or steep banks already formed be improved, and with open batteries behind them, and these first three towers added, the place would be secure. As long ago as 1873 the tower was described in a report on coastal defences as having defective brickwork, and it is now in poor condition. However, Folkestone Corporation, to whom it belongs, is about to start repair work.

*2 Houses and roads have crept towards this tower, which is on a knoll slightly more inland and 50ft below the first tower. In 1964 it was bought from Folkestone Corporation and has been converted into a dwelling. The exterior is painted white.

*3 This tower is on the cliff edge directly above Copt Point with a good view of the harbour. It is the one that figures prominently in the painting by Turner of Folkestone in 1830. Earlier in this century it was a dwelling and later was connected with the miniature golf links nearby.

*4 In common with the rest of the towers from here to the end of Shorncliffe Heights, this martello has a deep ditch; it is partly filled in and used as a kitchen garden. The tower itself is not occupied but stands in the garden of a private house at the extreme western end of the Leas. Inside the tower there is a slate water-tank on the ground floor. This was one of the towers fitted with a semaphore machine for sending messages in 1820; the others were nos 27, 31 and 55. During World War II no 4 was used by the Observer Corps.

*5 Here is another tower with its ditch laid out as a garden; it is in the grounds of the Girls' Technical School behind Sandgate High Street and off Coolinge Lane. It is in good condition and the inside is very interesting. There are two magazine compartments on the ground floor and the door of one of them is still covered with copper with details of the contents painted on it. There were plans in 1934 to turn it into a chapel for the school, but they never materialised. It is directly in line with Sandgate Castle which is on the shore below; this Tudor castle was brought into the South Coast tower project by Twiss who proposed throwing bomb-proof arches over some of the towers. The alterations were completed in 1806.

*6 Nos 6, 7, 8 and 9 are all in the Shorncliffe Camp area. When the martellos were built the barracks had been recently finished, but they were not the ones that are there now. Tower 6 stands on the outskirts of the camp; trees are growing in the ditch and there is a thick layer of soil on the roof complete with vegetation.

*7 Along with nos 8 and 9, this tower has been sealed by bricking up the door to stop further damage by vandals. No maintenance work is carried out on any of them and the exterior of this one is not in good repair. However, inside is a wooden floor laid in the original way with the boards radiating from the central pillar, but it is not known whether it is a replacement.

*8 This tower is abandoned in a bramble patch.

*9 The last tower in the camp area is in a fair state of preservation; almost all the stucco is in position and the brickwork of the ditch is in good order.

10, 11 and 12 These three were the first of the long line of low-level towers on the shore in front of Hythe. They were demolished during the last century when the promenade was made. No 10 stood near the present Imperial Hotel, no 11 near Saltwood Gardens and no 12 at the south end of Stade Street.

*13 At the western end of West Parade, Hythe, this tower was spared when the others were destroyed. It was sold by the War Department in 1906, and has been a dwelling since 1928. In that year it was bought by a Streatham builder, A. J. Glock, whose great ambition was to live in a martello. He carried out alterations and named it Place Forte. It changed hands in 1937 when it was bought by Edgar Wheeler. At the outbreak of World War II it was requisitioned and became an observation post for the coast artillery for shelling the French coast, clearly visible from here on a good day. The present owner, Mr Ronald Ward, FRIBA, the designer of the new lighthouse at Dungeness, bought it in 1960 and has since carried out a complete conversion. It is now known simply and properly as the Martello Tower.

*14, *15 and *19 These three towers stand in the middle of the flat land where the Hythe firing ranges are sited; it is a danger area used for rifle practice by the Hythe Small Arms School and Shorncliffe Barracks. Large capital letters, A, D and N respectively, are painted on the sides of the towers and relate to the letter given to the range in which each tower is located.

16, 17 and 18 These intervening towers were practically destroyed by the sea before the last war, but the ruins are visible.

20 and 21 Early in the present century these two towers had collapsed and disappeared.

The last group of towers in Kent were the three pairs built for mutual support to guard the outfalls of the Romney Marsh sluices. They were to the west of the redoubt and Twiss explained that they were to 'defend Dym Church Wall from an Enemy landing, and insure the opening of the Sluices, whenever orders may be given to that effect'.

Page 89 A south coast martello tower, no 24 at Dymchurch, Kent, restored in 1966 by the Ministry of Public Building and Works and open to the public

Page 90 (above) An east coast martello tower, an aerial view of tower W on Bawdsey Cliffs, Suffolk, showing the cam shape of the tower and the quatrefoil arrangement of the gun platform; *(below)* the doorway of martello tower F at Clacton, Essex, showing the stone quoining and the present drawbridge across the moat

22 and *23 This pair was built to protect Willop Sluice in Hythe Road, Dymchurch. Only no 23 survives, no 22 having been demolished by the Kent County Council in 1956 for road improvements. It was in a poor state of repair but needless to say proved exceedingly difficult to destroy; in the end high explosives had to be used. No 23 was described in 1948 by Commander Mead as 'looking as though the garrison had just marched out'. It is still in its unspoilt original condition inside and was used as a guide for the restoration of the interior of no 24. The Romney Marsh Rural District Council is about to undertake a full restoration of the exterior of no 23 at a total cost of £4,500 ($10,800); the money will be provided by the Ministry of Public Building and Works, the Kent County Council and the Rural District Council. The roof will be made watertight, the interior repaired where necessary and the surrounding area tidied up.

*24 and *25 Situated at the west end of Dymchurch village, these two guarded the main Marshland Sluice. They are now the last surviving pair of towers in this formation. No 24 was entirely restored by the Ministry of Public Building and Works in 1966. It is now open to the public during the summer months and there is a display inside the tower giving the historical background. Prior to this it was used by the coastguards for a long time. No 25 has also been restored but on the outside only. Before this work was done it was only a shell, but a new roof has been constructed in place of the old vaulted one.

26 and 27 This pair guarded the Globsden Gut sluice gates opposite St Mary's church; no 26 was demolished in 1871 and no 27, which was at one time a semaphore station, in 1841.

SUSSEX

The coastline of this county was martello country par excellence, but as most of the martellos were low-level towers many of them have been destroyed by coastal erosion and only ten are left. The forty-seven towers do not fall into such neat groups as those of Kent. However, with the help of the report made by Twiss on coastal defences and proposed tower sites on 3 September 1804, it is possible to get some order out of chaos even where the towers have long since disappeared and the coastline is greatly altered.

The towers started at Rye and three in that area guarded respectively the harbour mouth, the harbour and the sluices of the Royal Military Canal and the rivers Brede and Tillingham. The expanse of undrained marsh between the harbour and the beginning of Pett Level shore was, as Twiss observed, capable of flooding and contained the impassable 'great Morasses' so that towers were considered unnecessary. There followed a line of eight towers on the beach in front of Pett Level, built at approximately 600yd intervals, all of which have gone. The last of this line was at Cliff End, and from here to beyond Hastings no towers were built because, as Twiss wrote:

> ... the Land near the Shore is so high that Towers do not seem applicable to its Defence, and the accessible parts which are of small extent, compared to the inaccessible, may be strengthened, by escarping and Parapets, but must afterwards be defended by a movable force.

West of Hastings the towers began again and continued to the other side of Bexhill. Twiss described this stretch as '... in some degree protected by a rocky Shore, a rear Ditch and low Cliffs behind it...' With the exception of two cliff-top towers at Bulverhythe, they were all built on the shore below the cliffs. Not one of them remains today, twenty-four having disappeared between Rye and no 55 at Norman's Bay, the last of the twelve towers in Bexhill parish. The line continued in a sweep round the perimeter of Pevensey Bay, where the towers were all at low level and built directly on the shingle. They were at 600yd intervals and as well as protecting an easily accessible landing place, some of them guarded the Pevensey Level sluices. The last tower in this formation, in which five towers are still standing, was no 66 at Langney Point on the outskirts of Eastbourne. To the west of this point was the redoubt or eleven-gun tower at Seahouses. A mile inland and slightly to the east a solitary tower was built on St Anthony's Hill to protect the approaches to the fort. West of the redoubt, and nearer to Eastbourne, were five more low-level towers, all of which have disappeared, and finally on a little knoll towards the foot of the cliffs at Beachy Head was no 73, the surviving Wish Tower. The Seaford martello, added in 1810 and separated from the other towers by the downs and chalk cliffs, was built at low level in association with a battery nearby on the Buckle and a fort on the eastern-facing side of the cliff overlooking the mouth of the river Ouse and Newhaven harbour. A landing here would have given an enemy access to the town of Lewes and thence northwards to approach London.

Tower no

*28 The first Sussex tower at Rye Harbour was built on the west bank of the river Rother in a picturesque position on a small shingle knoll; to match this, it was given the romantic name of the Enchantress Tower. It stands in a dry ditch which has lost much of the soil forming the ramp at the back of the counterscarp on the east and south sides thus exposing the brick buttresses which strengthen it. There is a caravan and camping site close to it, and yachts tie up nearby. The building is in a shabby state and the moat is overgrown and has rubbish in it.

29 Abandoned almost as soon as it was built, this tower stood near the harbour mouth and was an early casualty.

*30 Standing as it does over two miles inland, it is difficult to think of this tower as a sea defence. Every other form of military defence had apparently given way to martellos at the time it was built. The tower stands to the west of Rye on the Winchelsea road and protected the important sluices of the Royal Military Canal and those of the rivers Brede and Tillingham. A battery stood to the west of it, almost half way to Winchelsea. It was a moated tower and one of the two equipped with a cunette or small wet ditch at the foot of the glacis. It was one of the very few towers in this range that was not in some way refortified during World War II and therefore nothing was added to the roof. Part of the drawbridge fixture remains, and at one time it was a dwelling and two small sash windows were added. It now stands in the yard of a scrap metal dealer. A picture of Rye by Turner shows this tower, but it is not easily recognisable as a good deal of artist's license was used. It is 20 miles before the next surviving tower is reached at Norman's Bay.

31 to 38 Eight towers were spaced at equal intervals on the two-mile stretch of coast in front of Pett Level; they were built directly on the shingle like the ones at the Crumbles near Eastbourne and sea erosion has swept most of them away. The first was at Dog's Hill and the last at Cliff End near Hastings, situated at the end of the extension of the Royal Military Canal that isolated Pett Level. Little is known of their subsequent history. At least three were blown up by the Royal Engineers because they were unsafe. These were no 37 in June 1864 and nos 35 and 38 in April 1872. As late as 1966

stones from a martello were found in the sand at low tide which, according to the position, would have come from no 36 or no 37.

39 and 40 Following the gap without towers from Cliff End past Hastings, these two were the first of four low-level towers which started at St Leonards and continued to Bulverhythe. Nos 39 and 40 were described as being in a 'critical position' in 1873 and were demolished soon afterwards. No 39 was on the west side of St Leonards; its site was near the swimming bath at West Marina. Its seaward side collapsed in 1876 and the Royal Engineers blew up the remains.

41 and 42 Built at the Salts, Bulverhythe, these two low-level towers had disappeared by 1842. By this date both had suffered damage from sea erosion and the Board of Ordnance decided to give them up and to sell the materials. It is said that they were demolished to make way for the London, Brighton & South Coast Railway line, but there is no mention of this in the War Office material in the Public Record Office and it is improbable that their sites would have interfered with the line which must have been built further inland. No 42 was demolished in 1840 and the materials were sold for £217 9s 6d (£217.47$\frac{1}{2}$) ($521.92). Some of the stone was used in building a chancel to St Mark's church at Cooden. Two years later no 41 disappeared in a flurry of legal language and wind! The materials were divided into thirty-three lots by a local auctioneer and the sale fixed for a day in February 1842. A builders' merchant from Hastings bought the first twelve lots, but when he went to collect them he was restrained by a notice from the freeholder of the land claiming that as the lease had not been surrendered, the Board of Ordnance was committing an act of waste. While the board was considering its next step, a gale split the tower in

two and swept it into the sea. Rather than take legal proceedings, the board repudiated the charge of waste, annulled the sale and refunded the price they had paid to all the purchasers, a total sum of £235 2s 0d (£235. 10) ($564.24) plus interest![1]

43 and 44 As a change from low-level towers built on the beach under the cliffs, here were two, both with dry ditches, on the cliff top overlooking Bulverhythe Bay. One was on Bulverhythe Cliff and the other on Galley Hill; they had both collapsed into the sea by the beginning of this century. They were the first two of the twelve towers in Bexhill parish.

45 From this point began a long line of low-level towers which stretched as far as Cooden and then merged into the Pevensey Bay line. Turner did a drawing of some of them in 1817 for his work 'Liber Studiorum'. He probably stood under Galley Hill looking westwards, in which case no 45 would have been the first in the line depicted. It was built to the south of the present Sackville Hotel and had disappeared by 1839.

46 Traces of this one were found in 1910 when the Colonnade was built; it was on the Horn and was demolished in 1870.

47 This tower was situated at the western end of the present Polegrove; there is no record of when it disappeared. On the local tithe award map of 1839 it is shown on the edge of the sea, but in 1844 it appeared in ordnance correspondence complete with a rough sketch of the base and some measurements.

48 The tower was built to the south of the existing Pages Avenue, and was demolished in 1858. There has been some controversy about the date when it was built because of alterations in the numbering of towers in a new printing of the 1in ordnance survey map of 1867. Up to 1854, when a new engraving of this sheet was

published, martello towers had not been numbered on maps and these were added to the plate along with a certain number of other sporadic revisions. By some error, either of fieldwork or in engraving, tower no 48 was omitted and all subsequent numbers were therefore wrong. This fault was corrected in the 1867 printing by re-numbering the towers by figures in parantheses; by this date no 48 was no more but its site was marked. The theory that martello building stopped for a time after Trafalgar is incorrect and it is clear from Twiss's letter to the oard of Ordnance of May 1808 that payment was made for seventy-three towers to the contractor (see pages 81-2).

49 Little is known about this tower; it was built near Veness Gap and had disappeared before the end of the last century.

50 This tower stood near the site of the present Cooden Beach Hotel. It was one of the towers used to test the superiority of new muzzle-loading guns over the old breach-loading guns by the Royal Artillery. The Duke of Cambridge attended the demonstration in March 1860. As his train approached Bexhill across the marshes, he was greeted by a royal salute fired by some of the Pevensey Bay martellos—a rather macabre and ironic gesture in the circumstances. The guns that were tested were 32-pounders and 68-pounders, fired from Cooden Down while a crowd of about five thousand people watched the proceedings.

51 to 54 These four towers were all on the shore in front of Cooden and had all been washed away by the sea by the beginning of this century.

*55 By some miracle, this tower has survived at Norman's Bay; it is close to the sea but in a fair state of preservation. It was one of the towers fitted with a semaphore machine for sending messages and, as if to perpetuate the tradition, it was used for a series of experiments in a system of wireless telegraphy invented by a Mr A. T. M. Johnson. With a solicitor from Eastbourne he formed a company and applied to the Postmaster General for a licence in 1905. The tower later became a private summer residence until the beginning of World War II.

56 to 59 These four towers carried the line as far as Pevensey Bay village and were built at regular intervals of 600 yards. The main Pevensey Level outfall was between 58 and 59. The first three towers were victims of sea erosion but 59 was demolished by workmen in 1903 to clear the land for a building estate. In July of that year a photograph was published in the *Navy and Army Illustrated* showing a large gang of navvies engaged on the operation and horses and carts waiting to remove the debris.

There is now a stretch of coast round Pevensey Bay where several towers are still visible and it is possible to get an impression of how they looked originally.

*60 A survivor standing in the village of Pevensey Bay close to the shore, this tower is in fair condition.

*61 This tower had a position-finding cell built on the roof during World War II. It is now the centre-piece of the new Martello Estate with lawns and stone paths laid out neatly round it and blocks of flats beyond. It was probably from this tower that Val Princep, a well-known marine artist at the beginning of this century, painted his wide-spreading seascapes.

*62 This tower has been used as a home for a long time, and is surrounded by caravans.

63 During World War II, the martellos were very much in the front line, both geographically and because many of them were used for military purposes, and this tower was blown up by the enemy.

*64 In an isolated position among the pebbles, this tower is still standing but is very near the sea.

65 By 1938 this tower had collapsed in ruins.

*66 This tower is close to the sea and a few yards east of Langney Point; it was one of the towers associated with the battery here. Just behind it is a service road that runs along the shore as far as the site of no 63. It is connected with the Crumbles Rifle Range and is used by the coastguards.

67, 69, 70, 71 and 72 This group of low-level towers ran along the coast from just west of Langney Point past the Redoubt, or eleven-gun tower, which is still standing, and into Eastbourne. It is not recorded how they all disappeared but no 71 was used as a target for the new rifled Armstrong guns by the Royal Artillery. This was in 1860, which was a great year for testing new guns and demolishing martellos at the same time. No 50 and no 68 were also victims of these tests. There is a photograph of the results of the bombardment of no 71 in Chambers' *East Bourne Memories*. It shows part of the parapet and wall beneath destroyed and the gun slide and pivot from the roof tilted at an angle.

68 Numerically misplaced in this list because it was a mile inland and to the east of the Redoubt, this tower's purpose was to protect the fort's landward side. As with no 30, it seems wrong to class it as a sea defence. It was built on the small conical St Anthony's Hill; in Twiss's original report on tower sites, he had not made up his mind exactly what type of 'enclosed work' was needed here and evidently a martello seemed to be the only answer. It suffered the same fate as no 71 being used as a target in August 1860 to test the new rifled Armstrong guns. It was finally demolished by fifty rounds from a 100-pounder, an 80-pounder and a 40-pounder at 1,000yd distance. Later a housing estate

was built on the site and the shape of the tower and its ditch is clearly visible in the circular arrangement of the buildings. The moat was filled in and is now a road, called the Circus.

*73 Probably the best known martello of all, the moated Wish Tower at Eastbourne was built on a little knoll overlooking the sea. It got its name from the nearby 'Wash' or 'Wish', a marshy piece of land near the outlet of the Shomer dyke, now Devonshire Park. The tower was used by the coastguards for a time after the Napoleonic wars were over, and towards the end of the last century it was abandoned and neglected and there was some agitation to have it demolished. However, the corporation leased the tower from the War Office in 1883 and let it to a family named Hollobon. It was run as a geological museum by them until the outbreak of World War II. It was during their occupation, when Eastbourne had become a seaside resort, that visitors to the museum adopted the custom of writing their names on the whitewashed walls inside the tower and wishing. Thus was the name justified in a popular manner! In common with most martellos, it was reclaimed by the War Office at the outbreak of World War II, and two 6in guns were mounted on the roof. Derequisitioned in 1947, the tower remained unoccupied and plans were put in hand to demolish it and build a sun lounge and café on the cleared land. Fortunately, in 1959 the Minister of Public Building and Works declared it an Ancient Monument after appeals from local residents and other interested people. Demolition work had already begun and the stucco had been stripped from the walls and part of the moat destroyed. The unhappy incident ended with a complete restoration being carried out on the building, although the corner of the moat was not replaced. The late Mr

Geoffrey Foyle, of the London bookshop, who lived in Eastbourne, gave £35,000 ($84,000) towards the work and the familiar landmark was saved. The Wish Tower is now open to the public and there is an interesting exhibition inside.

*74 Seaford Martello, added to the South Coast towers in 1810 and built with a moat, still stands on the beach, although as long ago as 1873 it was reported to be in danger of being washed away. The ramp or vallum on the sea side of the moat has been completely eroded exposing the brick counterscarp and the strengthening buttresses. Alterations that have been made to it may make it a little difficult to recognise, but underneath the superstructure that was added to it in about 1922 is the true martello shape. The War Office sold it in 1880 and until 1911 it was used as a museum. It was then bought by a local businessman who converted it into a café and amusement arcade, for which purpose it is still used. On the roof he added a six-roomed flat, the base of which projects over the original parapet. At some time before the Urban District Council bought it in 1948, the owner destroyed the drawbridge, replacing it with a covered platform over the moat and an addition to the counterscarp wall to turn it into a partly roofed shelter and promenade. Strangely enough, the last of the East Coast towers, CC at Aldeburgh, also had an addition built on the roof when it was turned into a residence before World War II.

A note to this chapter appears on page 165.

CHAPTER SEVEN

DISTRIBUTION OF THE EAST COAST TOWERS

Just as the martellos of Kent and Sussex were built to prevent the enemy reaching their ultimate goal of London from the south, so the towers of Essex and Suffolk were erected to stop their advance on the capital from the east and north in an outflanking movement. The part of the east coast that was protected by towers is flat and featureless and without the dramatic chalk cliffs of the south coast; the routes to London are also over flat country with no natural hazards or impediments. Once inland and north of the city, however, there were various military obstacles to contend with including a scheme to flood the Lea valley which had been carried out by Rennie before he started work on the Royal Military Canal in Kent in 1804. It was certain that landings from the invasion flotilla stationed in and around Boulogne would have been impossible, for it was a fair-weather fleet only, and to travel the distance through the Dover Straits and then northwards to the coast of Essex and Suffolk would have been a considerable undertaking. However, there was always the possibility that the barges could have been moved into the Low Countries and set sail on a perilous journey from that point, or that larger ships could have been used. The latter was the more feasible and it was probably because of this that the East Coast towers were larger and carried more armament than the ones on the south coast.

The coastline of Essex and Suffolk consists of a series of long river estuaries penetrating deep into the flat hinterland, the country between being low, flat and often marshy with swampy creeks, mudflats and islands. Where cliffs occur, they are low and would have been of no protective value against an invader. In the northern part in Suffolk long spits and banks of shingle are found. As early as 1797 Major-General John Moore undertook a survey of the area to determine the possible landing places for an invader and the works necessary for defence purposes.[1] Clacton and the surrounding area was considered to be the most vulnerable place in Essex, and there were already four batteries there. More were constructed after hostilities were reopened in 1803, and later when the towers were built, they were planned to support the existing batteries. As in other coastal areas, there was an outcry by local people for protection by towers as early as 1805, but it was not until 1808 that it was decided to build them here. Building began during the next year and by then barges blocked the entrances to the rivers Blackwater, Colne and Orwell and instructions had been issued for evacuating livestock.[2]

The towers were built to the north of the Thames estuary and its approaches—already protected by booms, barrages, land batteries and others mounted on anchored floating platforms—and began at the eastern extremity of the complex Blackwater estuary. They started at the mouth of the river Colne near Brightlingsea at St Osyth in Essex and continued as far as Walton-on-the-Naze. From this point the intricate channels of Hamford Water needed no added protection and nothing more was built until Harwich was reached at the mouth of the river Stour. A circular fort or redoubt, similar to the ones at Dymchurch and Seahouses, was started here in 1808 and there were two batteries. On the Suffolk shore opposite Harwich the towers began again and continued as far as Aldeburgh. The area contains the following estuaries leading to towns which were important route centres: the Colne to Colchester, the Stour to Manningtree, the Orwell to Ipswich and the Deben to Woodbridge. There is also the strange, shingle-girt outlet of the rivers Butley and Alde in the river Ore which had no major route centre at its head and only the little port of Orford on it. There were eleven towers in Essex of which six are left and eighteen in Suffolk with eleven still standing. Essex holds the doubtful record of being the county where a martello has been most recently demolished; this was tower B at St Osyth in the summer of 1967.

ESSEX

The first three towers commanded the entrance to the river Colne and are in the parish of St Osyth. These are followed by D, E and F on the coast from Jaywick and along the low cliffs in front of Clacton. Next came a line of low-level towers in front of Holland Marsh, G, H and I. The remaining two were one built on Walton cliffs and the other, K, a little inland overlooking the maze of inlets and channels of Walton Creek behind the Naze. All the towers but one, H, supported a battery, some of which, as has already been pointed out, were in existence before the towers were built.

The Essex towers were never occupied by troops, who were quartered at Weeley Barracks, built in 1803. The reason for this was a misapprehension about the climate on the east coast. An ordnance report of 1812, when the towers were almost finished, gives the explanation:

> ...as the unhealthiness of the Coast, would render it inadvisable to place troops in the Towers and Batteries till threatened with an attack. Fortunately Weeley Barracks are centrically situated ... and are within two hours march of any of the Towers and Batteries in this Quarter.[3]

This was stated despite the fact that Chatham, the Master of Ordnance, had written in September 1805:

The great object is to have the towers manned by persons who, by constant habit, should be at home in this business, and feel the sort of confidence that a smuggler has in his boat.[4]

(* denotes the martello tower is still standing)

Tower

*A The first tower was built at St Osyth Stone near Brightlingsea Ferry. It was used by the coastguards for many years and occupied by the army in World War I. Between the two world wars it was privately occupied and became a café. It still masquerades as one, and is known as the Tower Café serving the surrounding caravan camp.

B Built in a fine position on Beacon Hill, St Osyth and overlooking the river estuaries as far as Mersea Island, this moated tower was demolished in 1967 for a new housing development. The War Office sold it in 1908 and it was a private residence for many years. It was then used as a radio astronomical observatory by Mr F. Hyde until the time of its destruction.

*C This tower is close to the sea wall, at Bush Wall Point, and like some other towers on this coast, is in the middle of a caravan site. It has had a chequered career, and was sold by the War Office in 1906, becoming a dwelling for many years and later a refreshment room and a club. During World War II it was occupied by the army.

*D On the outskirts of Clacton, near to Jaywick, this tower was sold in 1904 and, with the land that surrounded it, became absorbed in a golf course. It is in fairly good order and the owners, Clacton Urban District Council, have leased it to the Secretary of State for Air.

*E Also in Clacton, this tower was built on Clacton Wash, an important position commanding an easy landing place with access to the main road inland, some twelve miles from Colchester. Like tower D, it was sold by the War Office in 1904, and in 1935 it changed hands and became part of Butlin's Holiday Camp. It is used as a water storage tower. It is in a fair state of preservation, and is now very close to the sea, standing on top of the sea wall.

*F A well-known landmark on the rising ground of Clacton Cliffs on the Marine Parade, the roof of this tower has been used by the coastguards as a lookout for many years. Shortly before World War II the interior was set up as a museum. It is now leased to the Defence Ministry and used by the Royal Naval Auxiliary Service. A report dated 1823 stated that its deep ditch was planted with wheat; today it houses a model village and zoo for children.

G, H and I These three towers, which guarded the Holland Marshes, were sold by auction with the land that went with them in April 1819 at the Bell Inn, Thorpe; they fetched £2,675 ($6,420) and they were pulled down immediately. The first tower was on a little hill near to the Sluice House, and its site is still known as Tower Hill; at the sale it realised £775 ($1,860). H stood in the centre of the present Frinton Golf Course; its materials were used for farm buildings at Kirby. The last of the three towers, I, was near Battery Point, Frinton.

J Built on Walton Cliffs, this tower and the land on which it and the associated battery were built was sold in 1835. It was in a dangerous position because of coastal erosion and was pulled down. The price paid was £1,255 ($3,012). It had a dry ditch which many years later was turned into the Round Garden at Walton.

*K Overlooking Walton Backwaters, this tower guarded

Martello tower CC at Slaghden, Aldeburgh, Suffolk, a unique quatrefoil tower and the last of a long line of English martellos. The structure on the roof was added before World War II when the tower was turned into a luxury residence; this photograph was taken in 1950

Page 108
Martello tower Q at Felixstowe, Suffolk, showing the extent of the moat, the outer wall or counterscarp of which has been cut through to make an entrance; this tower has no sharply defined glacis at the base of its walls. The castellations added to the parapet are an example of how a martello should not be altered!

Walton Creek and the marshes and inlets behind the Naze. In World War I it mounted a 24-pounder which remained in position for a long time. The land round it was for many years a camping site, and now it stands in a sea of caravans and is used as a bar.

SUFFOLK

The towers started again over the county boundary. In almost every case they were built to support a battery. The first three overlooked the confluence of the rivers Stour and Orwell opposite Harwich. Tower O was on the seaward side of Langer Point to strengthen the position of an old fortification, Landguard Fort. Tower P guarded the approaches from the north. There were then three more on the cliffs where Felixstowe is now, followed by another formation of three at the mouth of the river Deben. One tower, W, was on the low Bawdsey cliffs, and four low-level towers, X, Y, Z and AA formed a line of low-level towers at half-mile intervals on the shore from Bawdsey Beach through Shingle Street at the start of Hollesley Bay. BB was actually built on a shingle bank and with AA guarded the mouth of the river Ore. Finally, ten miles to the north the tower of Slaghden, Aldeburgh, commanded the river Alde where it turned south to join the Ore behind the long shingle bank which blocked its outlet to the sea.

Tower

*L and *M — On either side of Bloody Point, the tip of the peninsula between the rivers Stour and Orwell, two towers were built quite close to one another. L, the first one, overlooked the Stour at Shotley Gate, had a moat and supported a battery; the second, M, overlooked the Orwell. Both are now part of Shotley barracks, known as HMS *Ganges*, a Royal Naval training establishment. They are serving a useful purpose, L being used as a naval signals station and M is the base of a large water tank. They are structurally sound and the Captain of HMS *Ganges* comments that 'it makes one wonder why more modern structures cannot be built to last as long'.

*N On the opposite bank of the river Orwell, this tower faces M and is part of the three-tower formation. It is situated at Walton Ferry, now within the outskirts of Felixstowe. It supported a battery and was an interesting tower, having an exceptionally wide ditch and a cunette or smaller trench at the base of the glacis. The ditch was 70ft wide and the cunette, which was filled with water is 20ft, much larger than the only other one which was at no 30 at Rye in Sussex. The tower is in a poor and derelict condition.

O Considerable erosion on the tip of Langer point, where this tower was sited close to the old fort, has swept the tower away, but it was still there during the 1870s and appears on the Royal Military Academy copy of the OS 1in map of the period.

*P This tower is now at the western end of Felixstowe sea front, and is in reasonably good condition. It was built with a moat but this has been filled in at some time. The place where it stands is called Wireless Green and for many years it was the naval wireless telegraphy station communicating with destroyers going in and out of Harwich. The tower is now used as a coastguard station.

*Q Built in support of a battery at the south west extremity of Bulls Cliff, this tower has had many alterations done to it and it has been a private residence since 1946, when it was derequisitioned by the War Office and put up for sale. Up to that time it still had a drawbridge over the moat, but this has gone and the moat has become a garden.

R This tower stood half a mile from Q on the crest of the cliff at Felixstowe and had a moat. It was demolished earlier in this century.

S In a similar situation to R but half a mile further along the coast, this tower was abandoned in 1835 as unsafe. However, on the RMA sheet mentioned in the paragraph on tower O, its site is marked as 'Martello Place' and the plot of land on which it stood is still defined. On the shore in front of this is printed 'cement rocks', indicating that pieces of the tower were still visible.

*T and *U These two towers are at the mouth of the river Deben overlooking Woodbridge Haven. They are on low ground and T supported a battery. U was built a little further up the river mouth. The first tower is now associated with a golf course at Felixstowe Ferry and is used for storage purposes, but U is unoccupied and in poor condition.

V Built on the opposite bank of the river Deben facing U, this tower was part of a three-tower formation, and supported a battery. The land on which this tower stood was held from Lord Dysart on a ninety-nine year lease dated March 1810 at a rent of five shillings (25p) (60 cents) a year which could be terminated whenever it should cease to be needed for defence purposes. This happened, in fact, in October 1819, the Board of Ordnance retaining the buildings on the land. The tower was demolished almost at once, and the materials fetched £775 ($1,860), the same amount as those of tower G at Holland Marsh on the Essex coast which was demolished during the same year. Its circular site can still be seen in the grounds of Bawdsey Manor.

*W This was the second tower in Bawdsey parish and still stands on the low cliffs close to the sea. It is near to Off Farm and the patch of ordnance land in which it stood is well defined.

X Built on low ground at the southern end of Bawdsey Beach, this tower disappeared long ago but was still marked on the RMA map of the 1870s, mentioned in the paragraph on tower O. Its foundations formed the base of a gun emplacement during World War II.

*Y, *Z and *AA These three towers are all situated in what is the wildest and most deserted martello environment existing today; they run from Bawdsey Beach to Shingle Street and are close to the sea. Y was built in Bawdsey parish, Z near Buckanay Farm in Alderton and AA at Shingle Street, Hollesley. Y and AA supported batteries. They are unused but in fair condition.

BB This tower was on a shingle bank near the mouth of the river Ore and half a mile from AA. It was demolished in 1822 because it was unsafe.

*CC The strange ten mile tongue of shingle separated this tower from BB. It stands about a mile south of Aldeburgh at Slaghden and supported a battery on the outskirts of Aldeburgh. This tower is the most unusual martello in the British Isles. Shaped like a four-leafed clover, its design may have been influenced either by the south coast Tudor castles or by the quatrefoil shape of the East Coast towers' gun platform. It is also possible that this was the design for the four-gun tower planned for the east end of Dymchurch Wall but never built. This theory is supported by the fact that four 24-pounder guns were mounted on the roof. There was also a platform on the sea side of the tower on which guns were mounted. The tower was not stuccoed and it is presumed that it was never finished. There has been a great deal of coastal erosion here and this unique building is now dangerously close to the sea with shingle filling in the dry moat. In 1861 the tower keeper reported thus: '. . . built in an artificial circular dry ditch 50ft in diameter and 448ft in circumference. The tower is 40ft in height and the platform is bombproof.' In 1932 it was sold and turned into a 'luxury residence'. A sun parlour was built on the roof, a water supply was laid on and gas was generated on the ground floor for heat, light and cooking. During World War II it was occupied by the army, but it has not been used for a long time and is now in a sad state with the sea pounding its east wall and much of the outer skin of bricks falling off. There is a rumour that it may one day be lived in again by a sculptor who has been showing an interest in it.

Notes and references to this chapter appear on page 165.

CHAPTER EIGHT

IRELAND, JERSEY AND ORKNEY

The three groups of martellos on the fringes of the British Isles, in Ireland, Jersey and Orkney, include the first and last of them to be built in Europe. Ireland lays claim to being the first, building having started there a year before England, and the last tower was built in Jersey in 1837. The majority were built because of the Napoleonic wars, but the last five in Jersey were constructed when the application of steam to ships necessitated a reassessment and realignment of the island's defences.

IRELAND

If ever a country needed protection against invasion, it was Ireland. The French tried more than once to land there and one attempt succeeded (see Chapter 2). The conspiracy against the English was encouraged by the Society of United Irishmen whose leader, Wolfe Tone, plotted with the French in order to overthrow the government. From the French point of view, the main purpose of such tactics was to draw troops away from England, so that an invasion could take place on the south coast. The first French attempt was in December 1794, when an expedition under General Hoche sailed from Brest with some 18,000 troops on board. Bad weather wrecked the enterprise, separating Hoche's ship from the main part of the fleet which sailed into Bantry Bay in County Cork and anchored there waiting for their leader to appear. It would have been a formidable invasion had the troops landed, but the fleet sailed away without anything happening. Meanwhile discontent continued to grow in Ireland until rebellion broke out in May 1798. This was so relentlessly crushed by the English that when General Humbert and a French force landed in Killala Bay in County Mayo in August, the expected spontaneous risings never occurred and he found little enthusiasm for his cause among the local people. Nevertheless, the garrisons of England were considerably depleted to deal first with the rebellion and later with the French troops, who fought on Irish soil for seventeen days before they surrendered. Although other similar expeditions were planned for the autumn of that year, they never took place because the British navy dispersed the enemy at sea. There were no more attempts on Ireland by the French after this date, but with such a rebellious population the risk was still there.

As early as the beginning of January 1804 Lord Cathcart, the Commander-in-Chief of Ireland, wrote to the Ordnance Board:[1]

> My object is to construct some 'Battery's' [sic] with Towers or other works to defend them in the most expeditious manner at the entrance to Bear Haven—and that these works shall be defrayed as Field Works by Government and not upon Ordnance Estimates.[2]

At the time this letter was written the towers for the south coast of England were still under discussion and very little progress had been made. It was not until February of that year that the committee of engineers made their report to the cabinet on 'Towers as Sea-Fortresses'. It was September before Twiss proposed sites for the towers and October before a design for them was drawn up. In the early part of the summer of 1804 Twiss was in Ireland advising on a tower to be built on Whiddy Island in Bantry Bay, where the French fleet had anchored some ten years previously and therefore considered especially vulnerable. It is not certain, however, that Twiss played a part in the design of the Irish martello for the buildings on Whiddy Island do not come into this class and are correctly marked on the ordnance survey maps as batteries. There were three of these buildings but, except for the fact that they are circular, they bear no relationship to martello towers, although they were eventually thought of as such as this entry from a publication of 1837 makes clear:

> 1804 19 Oct A martello tower of unusual magnitude was constructed toward the N.W. point of Whiddy Island. Its interior diameter was 240 feet.[3]

It is more likely that the Royal Engineer officer in charge of building the Irish martellos, Lieutenant-Colonel Benjamin Fisher, was mainly responsible for their design. He had been Commanding Engineer in Jersey in 1798 and was in charge of the completion of the last of the range of towers on the island, La Rocca. The influence of the early Jersey towers may be seen in the one small machicolated gallery incorporated into the parapet above the entrance of the Irish martello towers. Strictly speaking, as the design for the Irish towers was settled several months before that of the English ones, they could have been dealt with in the chapter on the evolution of the martello design, but as the towers were so numerous—it is claimed that seventy-four were built to the same design during the course of the Napoleonic wars—they deserve a separate section.

Many features of these towers were the same as in the English ones, but they were in a simpler form, without such sophisticated engineering details as the eccentrically struck circles of the inner and outer walls. The Irish towers were uncomplicated, round buildings of unstuccoed blocks of dressed stone. In some respects they resembled the tower at Simon's Town. The walls were almost vertical with an overhanging parapet which sloped upwards to the crest of the building; there were narrow slits for musket-fire in the walls. The towers were approximately 40ft high, the walls 8ft thick and the entrance was 10ft above ground level. Projecting from the parapet above the entrance was a machicolated gallery, similar to the ones on the Jersey towers, for downward fire at any of the enemy who might try to force an entry. As in almost all martellos, the layout of the tower was on three floors. The ground floor contained a water tank and the magazine, which was known as the master gunner's store; the first floor was the troops' living quarters and the flat roof was the gun platform. Entrance was by a ladder to double iron doors at first floor level. Here was a single room without partitions, lit by two small windows and with a fireplace and cooking stove. In the wall away from the sea, a staircase led down to the magazine and another up to the roof. As with other tower magazines, as much metal work as possible was of copper to avoid sparks. The door was covered with a copper sheet and had a ventilator of the same material let into it. The door hinges and even the lock and key were copper. The walls of the magazine were lined with wooden battens to prevent the ammunition touching the stonework. The flat roof, which was surrounded by a 6ft parapet, had a raised emplacement in the centre with a pivot for the traversing gun. Most towers were armed with a single gun or carronade, but in more vulnerable positions one or two howitzers were added to the armament. It is interesting to see that, as in the Mortella Point tower, provision was made for heating shot, and two shot furnaces appear in the inventory of Sandycove Tower; it was the hot shot from the French guns on the Mortella Point tower that had caused most damage to British ships by frequently setting them on fire.

Because Ireland was considered to be in imminent danger

of invasion, plans for the towers were not delayed as they were in England. They were treated as fieldworks and building was able to go ahead without lengthy preliminaries. By the beginning of June 1804 plans were made for towers to be

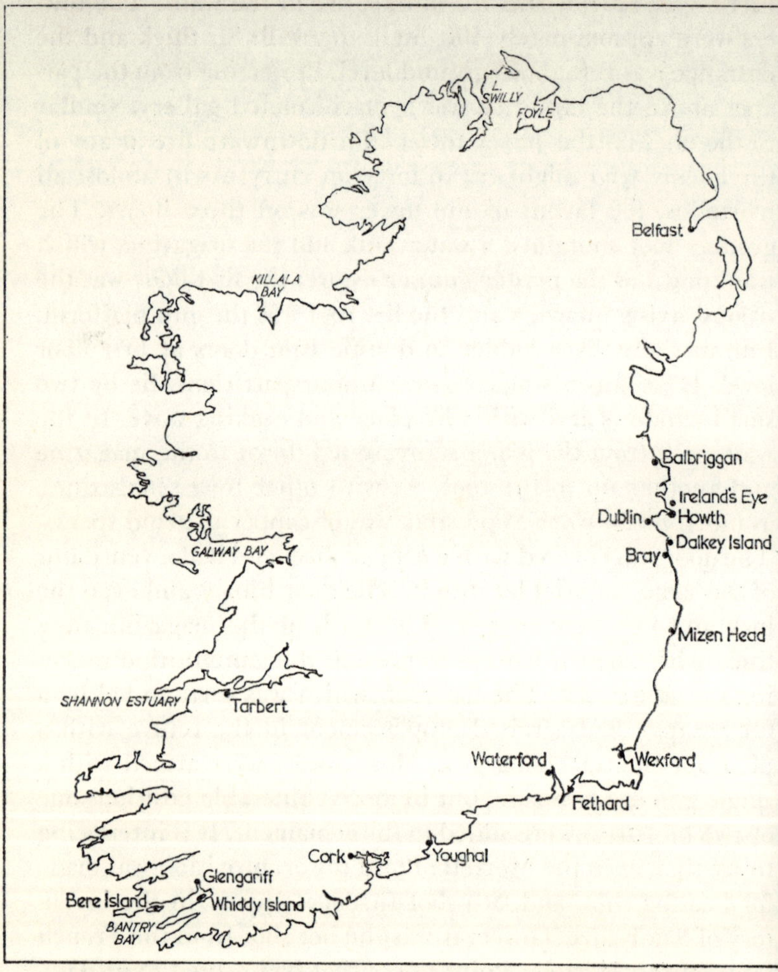

Ireland, showing the main places where martello towers were built

built on the eastern coast to protect the city of Dublin and by the middle of the month Lieutenant-Colonel Fisher received orders to begin the work. It was expected that each tower would cost £1,800 ($4,320) and their purpose was to 'co-operate in the Defence of the Coast, but [they] are principally intended for the protection of and as keeps to the Batteries'.[4] The first group to be planned was on the south side of Dublin Bay. There were to be fourteen of them, stretching from Bray Head in the south to Bathing Point at Seafort Parade near to Dublin itself. Two of the towers in the list, no 9 on Dalkey Island and no 14 at Seafort Parade, were in key positions and were to be equipped with two guns. In this first list, no sites had been chosen for towers 5 and 8, and when work began there were some changes in positions and the total was increased to sixteen. The original sites were listed as follows:

No 1 tower near Bray Head
No 2 tower on Bray Point
No 3 tower on the Strand near Old Cork
No 4 tower on projecting point in Killiney Bay
No 6 tower to the left of Loughlinstown river
No 7 tower on Tarrong Hill
No 9 tower at Dalkey Island
No 10 tower at Bullock
No 11 tower on Sandycove Point
No 12 tower at Glasstool
No 13 tower at Dunleary
No 14 tower at Bathing Point, Seafort Parade

More details about the towers were sent to Morse, the Inspector-General of Fortifications, by Fisher on 1 September. Eleven sites had been chosen 'for Immediate execution' on the north side of Dublin Bay—twelve were later planned—and more towers were proposed for the rest of the coast of Ireland. By this date the total had reached forty-four and included some at the entrances to the fine harbours of the south-west coast, which had already proved tempting to the French at Bantry Bay and where British troops sometimes embarked for the West Indies. The lonely coast of Galway Bay and the two great loughs on the north coast, Swilly and Foyle, were also to have martellos. Fisher's plans were now well advanced and he had managed to find a contractor.

> I have . . . enclosed a return of the Towers and Batteries which His Excellency the Lord Lieutenant has been pleased to order for the defence of the coast. The sites have been marked out to Mr Ross the contractor.

North side of Dublin, Howth to Balbriggan	11
South side of Dublin from Bray Head to Pigeon House[5]	14
Wexford, Fethard, Baginbun and Youghal	5
Oyster Haven	1
Bere Island	4
Galway Bay: Mutton Island, Newhaven and Finavarra	3
Lough Swilly	2
Lough Foyle	2
Belfast	2

This list and Fisher's letter must have arrived on Morse's desk at about the same time as Twiss's report and his proposals for tower sites on the south coast of England, which he wrote from Dover on 3 September 1804. Building went ahead in Ireland and by March of the following year—by which time work had only just begun on the English towers in Kent and Sussex—a report on the work in progress on the tower and battery on Garnish Island near Glengariff Harbour in County Cork was sent to Morse.

> The wall of the tower is built to within one foot of the height and the flooring joists are laid; the Contractor

Sketch map of the coastline north and south of Dublin showing the position of the martello towers

> states that the flooring Planks are prepared, but nothing as yet has been done to the Battery, Guardhouse or Kitchen. The Traversing Platforms are intended for the Battery and one in the Tower.

It was almost eighteen months, however, before Morse was informed that both tower and battery on this island in an extension of Bantry Bay would be completed on 14 August 1806. Building continued throughout the war and from time to time there were reports that work had ceased, but still in 1812 and 1813 towers were going up at Lough Swilly and Lough Foyle.

Of all the groups of towers in Ireland, the concentration round the capital city of Dublin was the most important. Of these, no 11 at Sandycove to the south of Dublin must be the best known martello among English speaking people. This tower is now the James Joyce Museum, and all those who have read his *Ulysses* are well acquainted with the building. Joyce stayed at the tower for a few days only in the summer of 1904 as the guest of his friend Oliver Gogarty, who had rented it from the War Office for £8 ($19.20) a year. Gogarty claimed that the reason for leasing the tower was to give the author the necessary seclusion for him to finish a novel. But the plan came to nothing; there was a clash of temperaments, and the uncomfortable incident ended in Joyce's departure. But although his visit was short, the tower evidently made a deep impression on him. When later he recounted the occurrence, with a certain shrewish delight, in the first pages of *Ulysses*, his description of the tower was tinged with romanticism; the tiny windows he called 'barbicans' and—through the lips of one of the characters—compared it with the castle at Elsinore 'that beetles o'er his base into the sea'.

The majority of the martellos were evacuated by the military by 1900. The armament of the Dublin Bay towers was removed in 1867 with the exception of three of them; one of these was no 11, Joyce's tower, which was equipped with a new 18-pounder rifle-barrelled gun. By 1900, however, this too was removed and the tower became obsolete and available for other uses.

The state of the Irish martellos today is similar to that of the English ones. Over the years most of them have been sold to private owners. Some, particularly those that were built on the shore or 'strand', have collapsed into the sea without trace and some have been demolished to make way for railways or modern buildings. Others have been converted into homes and two are used as cafés. The one at Howth, to the north of Dublin, has for many years been in the hands of the Department of Posts and Telegraphs and is the terminal for the cables under the Irish Sea.

Identification of the martellos or their sites is in some cases complicated for several reasons. Records are difficult to trace and surveys were not always accurate. Towers that disappeared long ago were often unmarked in any way. As in the Channel Islands, other defence works have acquired the name of martello over the years; these include ancient round towers, the three batteries already mentioned on Whiddy Island and signal stations, which were usually square and were built on headlands and islands between 1800 and the end of the war with France, particularly in the neighbourhood of Cork and as far west as Valentia Island. To complicate matters even more, since Ireland was divided after World War I, some place names in the Republic have been changed. Thanks to the co-operation of the Maritime Institute of Ireland, the Office of Public Works and the Ordnance Survey Office, the list that follows is as complete as possible.

The group of martellos round Dublin Bay was planned in two parts, the ones to the south of the city being the first. These were numbered from south to north starting at Bray. Those to the north of Dublin were also numbered from south to north, ending at Balbriggan. All the towers were disposed of by the government at various times from the end of the last century, except the one to the north of Dublin a Howth.

(*denotes that the tower is still standing)

Tower no

*1 The first tower was at Bray, Co Wicklow. It has been converted into a house and is in good condition.

2 This was the second tower in the parish of Bray, at Mountpark. It is the first of five towers following one another that have disappeared.

3 In the parish of Old Connaught, a tower was built at Cork Abbey. It was marked on a map dated 1836, and either fell into the sea or was demolished when the Dublin to Bray railway was built.

4 and 5 Two towers were built in Rathmichael parish, one of them at Maghera Point, but neither exists now.

6 This was the first of three towers built in Killiney parish. It was known locally as Shangannah and disappeared many years ago.

*7 The second tower in Killiney is at the junction of Killiney Avenue and Killiney Hill Road; it is in good repair and is used as a store.

*8 The third Killiney tower has been used as a house for about forty years, and an extension has been built on top; it has recently been on the market.

*9 Built on the rocky Dalkey Island, this tower was in a very important position and was one of the range of towers armed with two guns. It is in good condition externally, but inside the wooden floor has collapsed.

*10 There were three towers built in the parish of Monkstown; this one is at Bullock and is reported to be intact and in very good order.

*11 Sandycove Martello was built on a rocky promontory and is now the James Joyce Museum and in very good repair.

12 These towers were probably destroyed when the rail-

Page 125 (above) The Wish Tower, Eastbourne, Sussex, no 73; a recently restored martello, its damaged moat is used as an outdoor restaurant; *(below)* a Canadian martello tower, no 4 in rue de Lavigueur, Quebec, overlooking the St Charles river

Page 126 (above) Martello tower at Saint John, New Brunswick, showing the conical shingled snow roof; from a water colour painted about 1828 by Dr W. Hunt *(below)* the interior of the Saint John martello; this is the first floor or living quarters and shows the fine domed brick roof and the central column as well as the historical display on view to the public

and 13 way was built. From maps of 1820 and 1821 no 12 was at Glasstool (or Glassthule) and no 13 near the east pier at Kingstown harbour (Dunleary).

*14 The tower at Seapoint is intact and is used as a café.

*15 The Williamstown tower is also intact and used as a youth club.

*16 This tower is at Sandymount, and is used as a café.

The following towers were all to the north of Dublin.

*1 Three towers were built in the parish of Howth where a large headland projects into the sea at the northern end of Dublin Bay. This is the first of them, at Red Rock, Sutton, and is reported to be in very good order.

*2 Next to the Sandycove Martello to the south of Dublin, this one at Howth Harbour must be the best known; it has been used as the cable terminal by the Department of Posts and Telegraphs for many years and it is externally in good repair.

*3 This is the third tower in Howth, and was built on the island called Ireland's Eye, a very strategic position.

*4 and *5 Two towers were built in the parish of Portmarnock and both of them are used as houses. No 4 is on the north side of Portmarnock itself, close to the shore, and has an extension with a castellated parapet added relatively recently to the roof to give more living accommodation. No 5 is at Malahide.

*6 This tower is at Donabate in the parish of Balcarrick and is reported to be in good condition.

*7 On Portraine Point, this tower is also in good order.

*8 and *9 Two towers were built in the parish of Lusk, one at Rush and one at Drummanagh and both are reported to be in good condition.

*10 and On the group of islands called the Skerries, two towers were built. The one on Red Island still stands and is

*11 believed to be in good order, but no 10 on Shennick Island, which was built at sea level, is said to be in ruins.

*12 This is the furthest north in this range of towers, at Balbriggan, and it is in good order.

Moving north along the Irish coast from Balbriggan, the fate of the two towers at Belfast mentioned on the list sent by Fisher to Morse on 1 September 1804 is not known.

On the north coast, two towers were built in 1812 on Lough Foyle, one on either side of the entrance to the lough. One was at Magilligan Point, the other at Greencastle. The military withdrew from these towers in 1894 and the one at Greencastle later became part of an hotel. A little further round the coast six martellos were built on Lough Swilly in County Donegal in 1812 and 1813. There were three on each side of the lough and they were situated as follows:

Dunree Head — This was the first tower to be built on this lough. It was on a rocky promontory jutting out into the entrance from the sea. It was built behind a battery, and its garrison was one master-gunner and twenty-seven men.

Inch Island — This tower guarded the narrow waterway between Letter Kenny and Ramelton. It was built, along with the other four towers, in 1813 and all of them had batteries.

Muckamish — was near Rathmullan.

Neid's Point — was about two miles north of Buncrana.

Knockalla — was near Portsalon, at the entrance to the lough.

Rathmullan — was the last tower to be built.

These towers and batteries had an interesting history. In 1894 the defences of the lough were improved and, as well as a new fort being built, the batteries and towers at Dunree, Inch Island and Neid's Point were re-equipped, the work being completed in 1900. Later, the garrisons were withdrawn from Inch and Neid's Point before World War I broke out, but Dunree and the new fortress were retained and eventually passed into the control of the Irish government in October 1938.[6]

On the west coast, two towers of the original three planned have survived in Galway Bay; they are at Finnavarra Point and on Auchinish Island, both at the entrance to the bay. Further south, on the Shannon estuary, there appear to have been several towers, though none were on Fisher's 1804 list. The condition of one on Scattery Island is stated to be fair, while one at Kelherrin Point has partly collapsed. There was also one on Tarbert Island which was demolished in 1968 when a new electricity generating station was built.

On the south coast, Bantry Bay was the first place where towers were begun, and five were built as follows:

Bere or Bear Island	Four towers were built here and they are all standing; they supported a circular battery.
Garnish Island	This tower, near Glengariff, is slightly different in appearance from the others and was the first to be built (see page 120). It supported a circular battery on its eastern side. It is in good order and it has been reported that the traverse for the gun is still in position.

In County Cork, it is not clear whether the tower at Oyster Haven, planned in 1804, was built but in Cork harbour there appear to be ten towers, as follows:

Great Island	Three towers are reported here; one is on the north shore of the island, one at Belvelly Bridge and one near the railway bridge at Belvelly.
Ringaskiddy	A tower in very good condition is still standing here. This one and the three on Great Island are all confirmed by the Ordnance Survey Office.

Haulbowline Island	One tower in good condition.
Foaty Island	One tower in fair condition.
Little Island	The tower here is reported to be on the site of a new smelter plant, so that its future may be uncertain.
Rossleague	One tower in good condition.
Ashgrove	One tower in good condition.
Rostellan	This tower is believed to be a ruin.

Continuing eastward along the south coast, in County Wexford two towers were built north of Duncannon in the approaches to Waterford harbour and they are still standing. There is no trace of the tower planned for Fethard in the 1804 list, but the one at Baginbun Head is believed to be complete and is used as a house. Finally, on the east coast at Mizzen Head in County Wicklow a tower in a ruinous condition has been reported.

As well as this surprisingly long list of towers, others have been reported which may or may not be martellos. A few of them are marked on maps as ordnance towers—that is, a tower on which a gun could be mounted, but not built to the standards of a martello. A list of them will be found in the notes on this chapter. It is given in the hope that their true classification may one day be forthcoming.[7]

JERSEY

Despite the range of towers built at the instigation of General Conway, the Governor, on the coasts of this island between 1779 and 1804, martello towers were constructed here both during the Napoleonic wars and later in the nineteenth century. They were of local stone, and stucco was only applied to the walls of some of them later in order to keep out the damp. The design used was that of the South Coast towers, but those built later in the century resemble the East Coast towers in shape. During the first period three martellos were built on the south coast facing France. Work on these began in 1807.

(*denotes that the martello tower is still standing)

Tower site	
*Portelet	It must have been in 1807 that this tower was begun. By March 1808 it was ready for occupation except for drying out. A letter at this date from General George Don, Lieutenant-Governor of Jersey, asked for enough coal to keep a fire burning day and night in the tower for a fortnight in order that it should be ready as soon as possible to be occupied by a detachment of troops.[8]
*Noirmont	This tower was known as Tour de Vinde, and was probably begun in 1810 and finished in 1814.
*Icho	Built on a rock in St Clement's Bay, Icho Tower was started in the same year as the one at Noirmont. At the beginning of 1811 General George Don informed the Home Secretary, the Rt Hon Richard Ryder, that the tower 'is in sufficient forwardness to admit of a guard being mounted at it'. In 1923 it was sold by the War Department for £80 ($192) and is now retained by the island government as a navigational aid.

The last group of martellos to be built in Europe were begun in Jersey in 1834, having been planned two years earlier. There were five of them, three looking away from the Continent of Europe on the west coast and one each on the east and south coast. The west coast towers were on the flat shore of St Ouen's Bay. This was eminently suitable for enemy landings and there were already four of the earlier towers guarding it. These later towers were added to the north of the existing ones.

L'Etacq — The most northerly martello in St Ouen's Bay, this tower was almost certainly built in 1834 and was destroyed by the Germans during World War II.

*Lewis — This tower was also known as St Ouen 1; its other name is derived from the Commanding Royal Engineer in Jersey, Lieutenant-Colonel Griffith George Lewis. The date 1835 is carved on the door lintel. Four years later permission was granted for this tower, among others, to be rendered on the outside with stucco or cement because of the damp.

*Kempt — Also known as St Ouen 2, the tower was named after Sir James Kempt, Master-General of Ordnance from 1834 to 1838. His name is also associated with the martellos at Kingston, Ontario, as he was Governor-General of Canada a few years previously when the towers there were suggested. It bears the date 1834 and is used by the Sea Cadet Corps.

*La Colette — This tower was begun in 1834 and is on the south coast of the island not far from St Helier.

*Victoria — The last tower of all was begun in the year of the young queen's accession. It is in Gorey parish on the east coast of the island overlooking the bay of Petit Portelet.

ORKNEY

The Orkney Islands are situated off the northernmost headland of Scotland, separated from the mainland by the turbulent Pentland Firth. After America joined in the war in 1812, two towers were begun here but building was not completed until 1818, three years after hostilities had ended. The towers were situated on either side of the entrance to Longhope, at Crookness and Hackness, to protect this fine sheltered harbour where ships assembled to await convoy across the Atlantic. A far-ranging American frigate could have caused chaos had one entered these waters. The towers were built of the local Hoy sandstone and are still in a state of very good repair. There is a story that has been told for many years of a local family who received a monthly payment from the government for certain services rendered to the garrisons of the two martellos. They continued to be paid until the beginning of World War I when coastal defences were reviewed and it was realised that the towers had been disused for generations.

Notes and references to this chapter appear on page 165-6.

CHAPTER NINE

NORTH AMERICAN MARTELLO TOWERS

As martello towers are usually associated with Napoleon's intention to invade the British Isles, the existence of a number on the opposite side of the Atlantic in North America may seem both curious and surprising. The early ones in Canada were built by the British against the French. The later towers were the outcome of differences between Canada and the United States, first in the 1812 war and then the 'cold war' that followed it for much of the nineteenth century.

It is possible in North America to see a complete chronological range of towers from the earliest version at Halifax, Nova Scotia, to the final phase of the design which was reached in the building of the two uncompleted and complicated defence works known as martellos at Key West in Florida. Between these two extremes are examples of several different types, the finest being in Kingston, Ontario. Building was not on the vast scale of the English project. The United States adopted this type of defence late and their towers were built sporadically and to no set design. Between 1796 and 1870 fifteen towers were built in Canada and six in the United States. Of these, nine of the Canadian ones are still standing. Local preservation societies and the National Historic Sites Service of the Department of Indian Affairs and Northern Development have done much to keep some towers in good

North America showing the position of the martello towers built in Canada and the United States

repair. Canada was, in fact, a pioneer in this field. In the United States one of the Key West towers is under the protection of the local art and historical society and one in Louisiana is privately owned. For the rest, little is known of their history and less care has been taken of them. Only now is anyone about to undertake serious research into the subject.

Martello building in North America occurred in two main periods. The first was confined to Canada during the war with France, and began earlier than in Great Britain. Within this period there are three separate groups. The earliest was at the important naval and military base of Halifax and consisted of three early versions of the tower built between 1796 and 1798. These were followed by four erected during the Napoleonic era in Quebec, at a time when it seemed possible that the Emperor might make a bid to recapture the former French colony. These four towers were therefore going up at the same time as the English ones and conform closely to them in design. Finally, on the Atlantic coast, three towers were begun much later in the war. Two of these were at Halifax, one of which was started in 1811 and the other in 1814, while at Saint John, New Brunswick, a tower was begun in 1812, the year when America entered the war on the side of France. The second period included the remaining Canadian towers on the inland waterways of Ontario and the ones in the United States, all of which were built between 1820 and 1873.

The political tension between these two countries which led to this last period of building was long-standing and dated back to the American War of Independence. During that time, many colonists loyal to Britain moved out of America and into Canada, settling mainly in Ontario and the Maritime States. These 'Empire Loyalists', as they were called, were particularly bitter towards America. At the same time, there was a section of American extremists who considered the monarchical system of government in Canada as a blot on a republican continent. The war of 1812, followed by an indecisive peace treaty left the two nations no friendlier. The terms of the treaty, in fact, sowed the seeds of the crisis that eventually brought the two countries very close to war. In addition to this general uneasiness, America had embarked on a period of territorial expansion, a course which did little to appease Great Britain and led both countries to eye one another with growing suspicion and to take defence precautions. America spent millions fortifying her Atlantic seaboard and the Gulf of Mexico, while Britain built defences on the waterways into the heart of Canada and these conditions continued until about 1870. Among these fortifications were martello towers.

The United States planned and built towers at irregular intervals from 1821 and in widely separated places from Louisiana to South Carolina. Canada, on the other hand, concentrated the building of her last four towers in the years between 1846 and 1851 and all of them were at Kingston on Lake Ontario. They had been planned with other military works in 1828 and it was the Oregon Crisis that sparked off this final phase of tower building. This crisis was a frontier dispute that arose from the Treaty of Ghent at the end of the 1812 war. The boundary between the two countries was then fixed at the 49th parallel from the Great Lakes to the Rocky Mountains and, as agreement could not be reached beyond this point, it was decided that the vast tract of land known as 'Oregon Country' should be held in joint occupation. At the time the treaty was signed there were only a few white people in the area, most of them fur-trappers and traders connected with the Hudson's Bay Company. However, a number of settlers from the American mid-Western states later filtered into the territory and soon outnumbered the Canadians. By 1843 there was agitation in America, particularly in the mid-Western states, to annex the whole of Oregon, and negotiations were started with Britain to divide the rest of the continent across the Rocky Mountains to the Pacific Ocean at the 49th parallel. These were unsuccessful and broke down mainly because the British were unwilling to give up Fort Vancouver, which was situated south of the proposed boundary. In the following year a new president, the expansionist Polk, took office and the situation became more serious. Friction between the two countries increased, especially as some Americans hoped to gain the whole Pacific coastline as far north as the Alaskan frontier, thus depriving Canada of any outlet to the sea on the western side of the country. By the time negotiations were reopened in 1846, Fort Vancouver, the previous stumbling block, had been moved to the island of the same name and the American president accepted Britain's suggestions; these were for the international boundary of the 49th parallel to be extended across the Rockies as far as Puget Sound and there to dip southward to include Vancouver Island inside Canada. When these terms were debated in the Senate, the expansionists coined the slogan 'Fifty-Four Forty or Fight', meaning that they wanted American territory extended as far north as the Alaskan border which was on latitude 54° 40′. Despite this opposition the Senate accepted the new boundary and the Oregon Treaty was signed. This was probably because America was already at war with Mexico and was about to open hostilities against California. A third war, with Canada, would have stretched their resources to the limit.

The Key West martellos were built to guard the entrance to the Gulf of Mexico and strengthen the approaches to the United States' recently acquired territories in this area. Between 1803 and 1845 they had come into possession of Louisiana, Florida and Texas and thus controlled all the northern coastline of the gulf. The fortifications at the tip of Florida were an ambitious project planned to turn Key West into a second Gibraltar, thus threatening the entry of anyone into these waters. Britain, in particular, had cast covetous eyes on Texas.

CANADA

The Canadian towers had several interesting and individual features. Most were equipped with snow roofs because of the severity of the climate and the consequent damage to the fabric. These roofs were conical structures built over the gun platforms; some were made of shingles or boards and some of slates. The first reference to them concerned the Prince of Wales Tower which had a shingle roof in 1824.[1] The later Ontario towers had snow roofs built in triangular sections fastened together with cables which were anchored to a peg in the centre of the flat roof. In case of action, the sections could be dispensed with by striking a blow with a sledge hammer on the peg thus releasing the segments which slid over the parapet into the dry ditch below. The caponiers were another feature; these were covered projections built into the moat from the base of the tower, their walls having loopholes for musket fire to provide flank defence. They were first used on the Duke of Clarence Tower in Halifax in 1798, but their design was different from those built on to the later Kingston towers.

As well as being a pioneer in the use of martellos, Canada had the distinction of being the last country in the British Empire to build them. More important still, she was the first country to show concern for their fate and to take steps to preserve them. As early as 1925 Murney Tower in Kingston had been opened as a museum, having been taken over shortly before and restored by the local historical society. After a long pause, this was followed by Fort Frederick Tower which was repaired and opened as a museum in 1958. The Prince of Wales Tower in Halifax was restored and opened in 1962 and the following year the tower at Saint John, New Brunswick, was also opened to the public.

In Chapter 3 the three early towers at Halifax were described in some detail. As to their further history, the first, the Prince of Wales Tower, after more structural alterations which ended in 1862 and included the addition of four machicolated galleries, became obsolete, and was abandoned. For years the people of Halifax pressed for it to be preserved and finally it was declared a National Historic Site and a complete restoration was carried out by the Department of Indian Affairs and Northern Development; it is now open to the public and houses an exhibition. The two other towers were practically destroyed before the end of the century, both being reduced to the lower floor only. The Duke of York's Tower was used as a signal station from the time it was built until 1879, when telegraphic communication was established between the forts; it had relayed messages between Camperdown and the Citadel. Soon after it had ceased to carry out this function, its upper storey was badly damaged by fire, and by about 1892 all but the lower part of the tower had been demolished. This portion did duty for a time as a coal store. The Duke of Clarence's Tower, the only one of the three to be built with three storeys, had its upper floor removed in 1869 and was again reduced in height twenty years later; this truncated fragment was used as a barracks and magazine for a time until it, too, was swept away.

Although not in strict chronological order, the two other Halifax towers are more logically dealt with at this point rather than later in the chapter. Both were designed by Captain Gustavus Nicolls, and the first to be built was Fort Charlotte Tower, begun in 1811 and finished during the next year, when America had entered the war. It stood inside the fort on George's Island, a key defence position. The island is close to the peninsula on which the Prince of Wales Tower stands. By 1877 it had disappeared without trace when reconstruction work was taking place on the fort. There are few details known about its appearance, but it was 30ft high and its base diameter was between 45ft and 50ft.

Last of all the Halifax towers was Sherbrooke Tower,

started in 1814 but not completed until 1828. As a change from royal names, it was called after the Lieutenant-Governor of Nova Scotia at the time it was begun, Sir John Coape Sherbrooke. It was built at the end of a long spit of land jutting out from McNab's Island, facing York Redoubt and overlooking the channel into the inner harbour. While the other towers were constructed of either the easily worked ironstone or sandstone, this one was faced with granite blocks over the inner brickwork and was therefore considerably stronger than the rest and considered to be entirely bomb proof. However, the cost of building and quarrying the material was greater than expected and this, and the fact that the war ended in 1815, brought the work to a halt at the second storey. Ten years later work was resumed and it was finished in 1828; the result was a combined martello and lighthouse, a strange union of martial and humanitarian uses. The reason for this was that a lighthouse was needed on MacNab's Island and it was impossible to find a site where it would be clear of the martello's guns if they ever came into action. The provincial government and the military agreed that the light should be dismantled in a military emergency and that the civil authority should build and maintain a roof over the gun platform and place a cupola for the light on this. When a new lighthouse was needed after World War II, the whole structure was pulled down. All that remains are a few scattered granite blocks near the site.[2] The dimensions of the tower were:

height	32ft 7in
base diameter	50ft
thickness of walls	7ft 6in

The light added almost 7ft to the height of the tower. The ground floor housed the usual magazine and water tanks, the first floor had four 24-pounder guns for firing through gunports and on the roof were three 24-pounder long guns.

Meanwhile, a group of martellos had been started at Quebec before the last two Halifax towers were built. Begun in

1805, all but one of the four towers were finished by 1811. The design is very similar to the English South Coast towers, but they were constructed of unstuccoed stone. This line of towers was considered necessary in case of a French attack; a scheme of new defences was put forward for the town but the full programme was not carried out immediately. Quebec is situated on a rocky promontory between the rivers St Lawrence and St Charles; behind the town then was open country, the famous Plains of Abraham, the site of Wolfe's battle in 1759. The towers were spaced out in a line across this area between the rivers to guard the town from a landward attack as well as one from the rivers. Tower no 1 overlooked the St Lawrence from the old battlefield and was close to Wolfe's redoubt; no 2 was 600 yards further inland, and is now on Avenue Laurier near the observatory. The line has been broken at the next point as no 3 was demolished early in this century to make way for one of the buildings of the Jeffery Hale Hospital on Avenue Turnbull. The last of the line, no 4, was built in a commanding position on the edge of the Coteau Ste Genevieve overlooking a possible landing place by the St Charles river. This one was begun rather later than the others and was not finished until 1823. It stands in Rue Lavigueur and houses the Quebec Astronomical Society's telescope. From a plan of the town and fortifications made in 1808 it is evident that at least eight towers were planned, for tower no 8 is marked just outside the wall of the citadel overlooking the St Lawrence.[3] It would appear from this that a second line was to be built in echelon formation behind the first line of towers. The Royal Engineer officer in charge of the building of these martellos was Captain John By, later to become famous for constructing the Rideau military canal from Kingston to Ottawa or, as it was originally called in his honour, Bytown.

The tower at Saint John, New Brunswick, was the result of America's entry into the war in 1812. It was placed in a commanding position at Lancaster on high ground to the west of

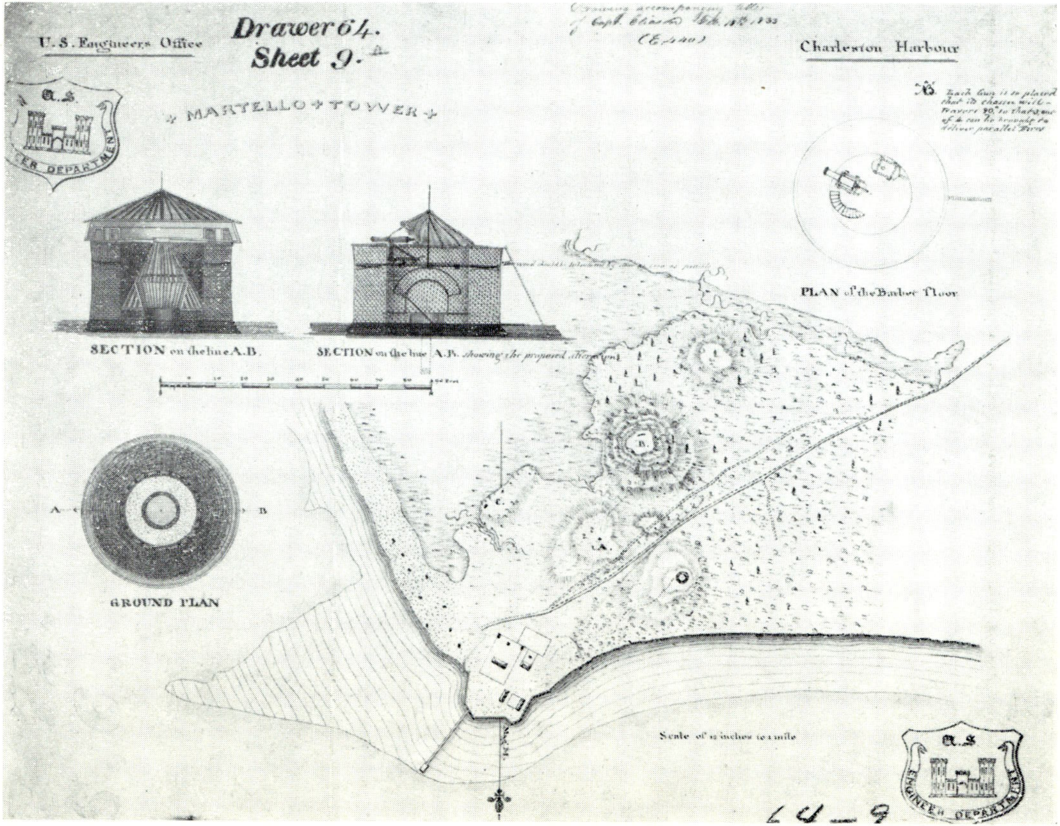

Page 143
Martello Tower, Charleston, South Carolina, USA, from drawings made in 1833 when repairs and alterations were suggested

Page 144 (above) Fort Frederick Tower, Kingston, one of four martello towers built on Lake Ontario between 1846 and 1851; this tower is now the museum of the Royal Military College; *(below)* martello tower, Tybee Island, Savannah, Georgia, USA; from an old but undated photograph. The door to the ground floor really excludes this tower from being classed as a martello, although it was one in purpose

the harbour; the strategic importance of the site was appreciated by later generations as emergencies arose. In World War II an extension was added on the tower's flat roof; this was the fire control centre for the harbour defences and here, also, all shipping movements in the area were received and plotted. Both the modern addition and the old martello are now used as a museum and it is classed as a national historic site. The tower was constructed of large, irregular sized blocks of stone, the central pillar and vaulted chamber inside being of English brick, some 78,000 having been imported. Its dimensions and general layout were similar to the English South Coast towers but the arrangement of the armament was different. On the first floor were gunports for two 12-pounder carronades; on the ground floor an area was walled off for the magazine, while the rest of the exterior wall was pierced with a number of gunports for musket fire, beneath which a firing platform was erected. The roof mounted two 24-pounder long guns and two carronades of the same calibre; it was covered with a conical snow roof of slate which was later replaced by pine shingles.[4]

Between 1846 and 1851 a group of four martellos was built at Kingston on Lake Ontario, the first of the series of Great Lakes and many miles from the sea. The area had been the main theatre of war with America from 1812 to 1814, with battles between fleets with ships as large, and larger, than Nelson's *Victory*. Kingston occupies one of the most strategic positions in the country, standing at the head of Lake Ontario where it narrows to form the St Lawrence river as it makes its way to the sea. It is therefore the gateway to the west, controlling the routes to the vast prairies, the Rockies and the Pacific beyond. Other important natural routes converge here, some by land and some by water; the Mohawk to the east leads to the river Hudson and New York while the Ohio valley is the way to the Mississippi and the Gulf of Mexico. The four martellos formed a semi-circular cordon covering the entrance to

Kingston harbour and the beginning of the Rideau Canal. This canal provided a protected way inland from Kingston to Montreal by way of Ottawa, thus by-passing the upper reaches of the St Lawrence where the American frontier faced Canada across the river. In time of war, this stretch of the river would have been almost impassable. Begun in 1827, the canal was finished by 1832; its construction was under the supervision of Lieutenant-Colonel John By. He had some interest in the Kingston towers also for he was a member of the Defence Committee which suggested three towers, among other works, 'to command a hollow way by which the Dock Yard could be approached'. These recommendations were endorsed three years later by a subsequent committee headed by the Governor-General of Canada, Sir James Kempt, whose name is associated with one of the martellos built in Jersey a few years later. The lesson of the 1812 war with America had been learnt, the importance and vulnerability of Kingston was recognised and a plan was put forward for six forts and four martellos to be built. Work started on Fort Henry and among the many constructions were two ditches running downhill from it to the water's edge. At the end of these, two small round towers were built. The ditches were made in 1840 and the towers were probably built at the same time. In effect and purpose, these towers were martellos but because of the large size and armament of the four main towers, they are rarely accepted as such and are usually classed as watch-towers. However, they could each accommodate eighteen men and mount a 24-pounder carronade on the roof. The walls of the towers were vertical and the exterior and interior circles were struck eccentrically with the thickest wall facing the water in the accepted manner. They were equipped with dry ditches and caponiers on the waterside. Whatever they are called, they should not be forgotten in the martello story as they are a true link with the original uses of martello towers.

As to the four main martello towers, they were begun in

1846 when, as has been pointed out, the Oregon Crisis made war with America seem inevitable. References to them appear, however, before that date in War Office papers, when they were referred to by letter only.[5] Sites had been selected and costs estimated by 1841; all of them are still standing and their positions are as follows:

Murney Tower, the most westerly, on the lake shore at Murney Point in Macdonald Park.

Cathcart Tower, on Cedar Island opposite Fort Henry.

Fort Frederick Tower, in the grounds of the Royal Military College of Canada at Point Frederick.

Victoria or Shoal Tower, which stands in the water of the harbour.

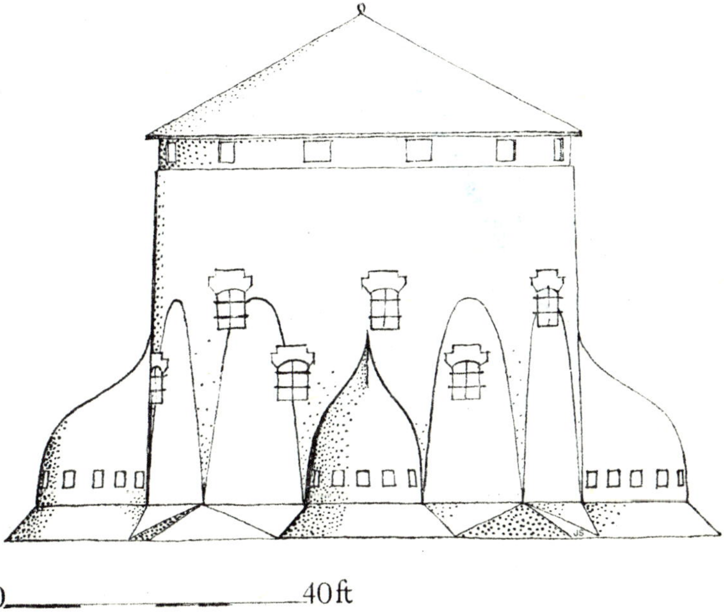

Elevation of Fort Frederick Tower, Kingston, Ontario, redrawn from architects' plans produced at the time of the tower's restoration

Generally speaking, the towers are similar in design and were constructed under the supervision of Lieutenant-Colonel Sir Richard Bonnycastle. They were built of limestone blocks with wooden snow roofs covering their gun platforms; these have been described on page 139, and the present ones are replacements and are permanent fixtures. The walls are almost vertical and in plan the towers are true circles but with the interior and exterior circles eccentrically struck, giving a

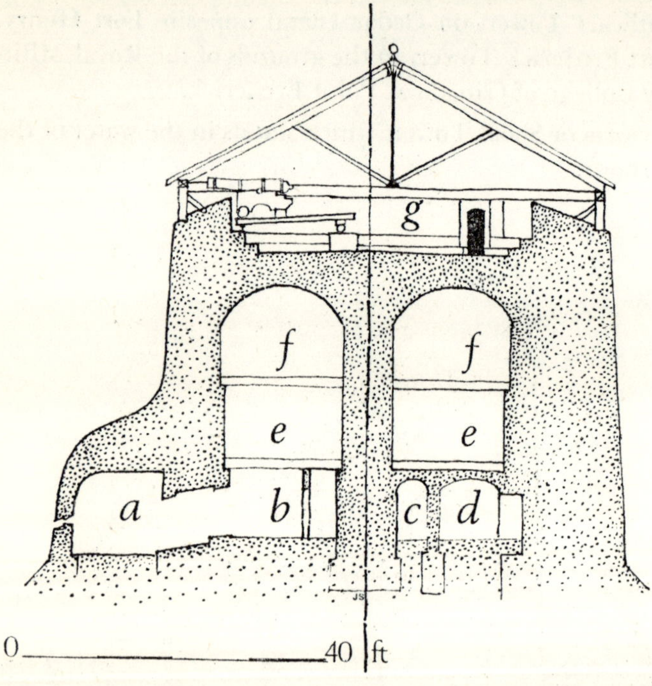

Sections of Fort Frederick Tower, drawn across line A-A in drawing on page 149:

a	*caponier*	e	*gunports on first floor*
b	*ordnance store*	f	*gunports on second floor*
c	*closet*	g	*flat roof, the gun platform, three guns*
d	*powder magazine*		

greater thickness of wall towards the water as in the English towers. The arched roof was beautifully constructed of wedge-shaped stones, a safety device which would have avoided its collapse had the tower been hit during a battle. Even if the mortar were shaken loose, the force of gravity would make the stones lock more tightly than before.[6] Three of the towers were of the usual form with two floors and a flat roof, but Fort Frederick Tower had an extra storey; it could house one officer and forty-eight men while the others held an officer and

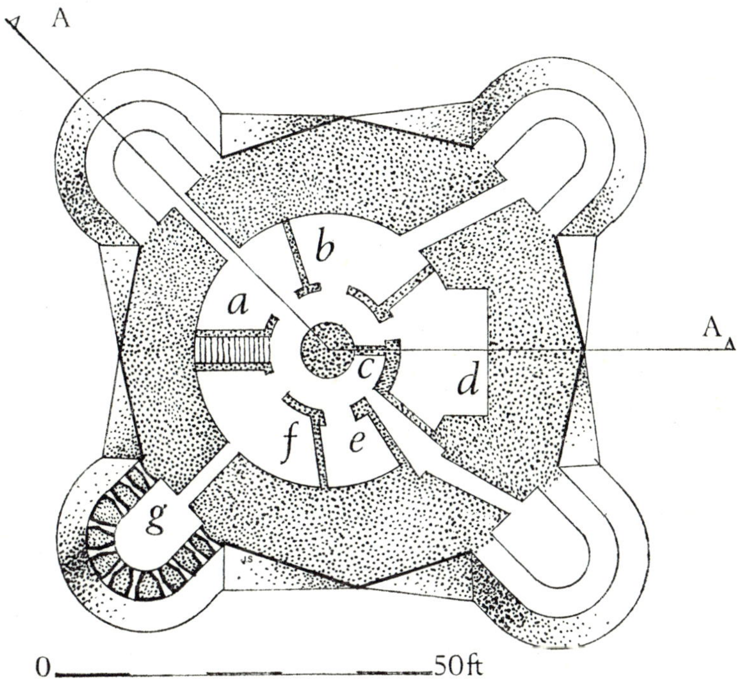

Ground floor plan of Fort Frederick Tower :

a	*ordnance store*	e	*artillery store*
b	*barrack store*	f	*commissariat*
c	*closet*	g	*caponier*
d	*powder magazine*		

J*

twenty-four men. With the obvious exception of Victoria or Shoal Tower, the other three had dry ditches and caponiers, known locally as 'chicken coops'. They are small loop-holed chambers with semi-circular ends jutting out from the base of the tower into the moat. To guarantee a supply of drinking water in case of siege, these towers collected rain-water on the flat roof which was piped to tanks on the ground floor just as had been done at the Mortella Point tower. On its way down, as an added refinement, it was boiled on the kitchen ranges; the steam from the cooking pots was also collected, condensed and piped to the tanks. The towers were armed with three 32-pounder guns on dwarf traversing platforms and raised racers on the flat roof, and on the first floor there were three 32-pounder carronades to fire through gunports. Fort Frederick Tower, having one storey more than the others, had three 32-pounder carronades as well on the second floor.[7]

Each tower has its special point of interest. Murney Tower was built in record time; the contract was awarded at the end of January 1846 and on 10 June a detachment of artillery placed cannon on the masonry to test its strength. This was an incredible achievement as no building work could have been undertaken during the long hard winter. The tower was originally named after the Master-General of Ordnance, Sir George Murray, and this name was cut into the stone above the door. At the same time Murney Point—named after a previous owner of the land—was to have its name changed to correspond with the tower built on it. But the similarity was too confusing and the old name lingered on. Eventually a metal letter 'n' was placed over the second 'r' in Murray on the tower, and the strange hybrid word 'Murnay' remains for all to see. This tower was the first to come into the hands of preservationists; in 1925 it was leased from the federal government by the Kingston Historical Society and after extensive repairs, it was opened as a museum. It had been obsolete and abandoned since the end of the last century until a violent storm brought its neglected condition forcibly to the notice of the city and its inhabitants. During the storm, a child was killed when some of the roof collapsed.[8]

The largest martello, Fort Frederick Tower, protected the site of the Navy Yard and the entrance to Navy Bay. It was built behind the earth works of an existing battery and the whole position was strengthened by a stone curtain wall and redan. Among the workmen employed on the tower as a stone mason was Alexander Mackenzie, who later became Prime Minister of Canada. During his term of office (1873-1879), the Royal Military College of Canada was opened at Fort Frederick and the tower now houses its museum. Until 1958 it was in a decaying condition, but it was then renovated and put to this new use and is visited by thousands of tourists during the summer months.

Cathcart Tower on Cedar Island faces Fort Henry across Hamilton Cove or Deadman's Bay; on a plan of the fort and its surroundings dated April 1870, the following details were written about this tower:

> tower built 1848
> cost £9,430 ($22,632)
> one officer and 24 men
> 1st floor 3 - 32pr carronades
> top platform 3 - 32pr guns

Like the Victoria or Shoal Tower, its condition has deteriorated and it is unused. Cedar Island, which is a delightful spot, is now a small provincial park administered by the Ontario Department of Tourism and Information, and it may be that some function will be found for it. The tower was named after the Commander-in-Chief of Canada at the time it was built, Lord Charles Murray Cathcart, whose father had held the same position in Ireland at the time the towers were being built there.

The construction of Victoria Tower actually in the harbour

water was an engineering feat. During the winter months of 1847 a coffer dam was prepared on the ice and when the spring thaw came, it sank into position. Pumping began at once and by the middle of June the inside of the dam was clear and building began. It remains as a conspicuous and unique feature of the harbour and, although it is not put to any use at present, there are rumours that it may be converted into a restaurant.

The completion of the Kingston towers brought to an end the building of martellos in the traditional form of a circular detached tower. Although their purpose was the same as before, the last three to be built in the United States were square or rectangular and the ones on the island of Key West in Florida were placed inside a rampart and battery.

UNITED STATES OF AMERICA

The American towers were few and far between and were not built to any set standard or design. Among the six built, there was a variety of shapes: they were round, hexagonal, rectangular and square.[9] Although called martellos, in many respects they did not measure up to the standards accepted in Britain and some would be better described as block-houses. The first three were planned in 1821 and consisted of two on the Atlantic coast and one on the Gulf of Mexico. Five more were planned in 1845, all on the Gulf of Mexico, but of these only three were built and not all of them were completed.

The two Atlantic coast towers were both built on islands; one was on the James river at Charleston, South Carolina, and the other at the mouth of the Savannah river in Georgia. Both towers were circular and had similar dimensions. They also had conical roofs like the Canadian towers, though they could not be described as 'snow roofs' but were intended to keep the rain from the wooden gun platform and parapet. The Charleston Martello, which was probably the first to be built soon after 1821, was opposite Fort Johnson. It is now a heap of ruins and almost unapproachable. The plans of the tower show it to have been of stone with an overhanging wooden parapet. There was no central pillar to support the flat roof, but instead there was an unwieldy construction of radiating beams not unlike the spokes of an umbrella. The dimensions of this martello were:

height	38ft
base diameter	52ft
thickness of walls	10ft

As early as February 1833 repairs and alterations were needed and some drawings which accompanied a letter on the subject from a Captain Eliason give some interesting details.[10] As with the earlier Canadian towers, the flat wooden roof and parapet had rotted and a note on the plan stated that 'The wood should be substituted by stone as soon as possible'. This alteration included lowering the flat roof, or barbette floor as it was called, and using the existing stone wall as a parapet, thus reducing the total height of the tower by 8ft. At the same time a strange tent-like roof of canvas was proposed to replace the conical wooden one. Four guns were to be mounted on the new gun platform or barbette floor, each to traverse 90°, 'so that 3 out of 4 can be brought to deliver parallel Fires'. Access to the roof was by a ladder propped against the outside wall. It is not clear whether these alterations ever took place. A drawing done in 1846 shows the building looking the same as it had done in 1833.

The Tybee Island Tower at the mouth of the Savannah river was also of stone with dimensions almost identical to the Charleston martello. An interesting document in the National Archives of the United States gives plans of the tower's four floors, surveyed and drawn by Lieutenant Mansfield with a memorandum dated 24 January 1845.[11] By this date the building was being inspected to see if it could be repaired and used. The tower was built of 'a composition called Tabby or

Tapis composed of shells and lime and is one connected and solid mass... The nature of Tabby is such that this Tower is gradually wasting away and every wind...leaves evident marks on one's clothes of the inutility of erecting permanent buildings, so called, of such material. Fortunately in this case, the walls are thick, and sound, and will stand for years and answer the purpose intended.' On page 144, an old undated photograph of the tower illustrates the point Lieutenant Mansfield wished to make about the durability of this soft limestone.

The memorandum continues with a brief description of each floor. The ground floor was the magazine and from it rose a hollow brick column which continued up through the whole height of the tower in the same way as in the Prince of Wales Tower at Halifax; it may have been used as an ammunition hoist and was thought originally to have terminated in a well. Although in purpose and essence a martello, this tower broke the essential rule by having not only a high level entrance door into the first floor but also one at ground level into the magazine, and strictly speaking should not qualify. Obviously a land attack was not considered possible. Internal stone stairs led from this floor to the first or entrance floor, and thence to the second floor which had three fireplaces and twelve loopholes for firing through. The gun platform mounted one gun on a pivot and the overhanging wooden parapet was provided with twenty-one loopholed machicolations. By 1845 this parapet was reported to be completely rotten and the conical wooden shingled roof which covered the platform needed renewing despite the fact that it had only been erected within the previous ten years.

The subsequent history of this tower is interesting, for it played a part in the American Civil War (1861-1865). Tybee Island was occupied by Federal troops who besieged Fort Pulaski, Savannah and a battery was mounted on the tower's roof. It later became the headquarters of the Georgia Telephone and Telegraph Company and was finally destroyed by government orders just before World War 1.

Tower Dupré was one of two martellos built in Louisiana to the east of the Mississippi river on Lake Borgne, an inlet from the Gulf of Mexico penetrating deep inland among the salt marshes and swamps of the great river delta. They were intended to prevent a repetition of an attack on New Orleans from this direction as had happened in 1815. On that occasion the barges carrying the English invaders had passed close to Bayou Dupré, the marshy river outlet on the western shore of Lake Borgne some ten miles east of New Orleans, where this martello was later built.[12] Plans for it were submitted to the secretary of war by a board of engineers in 1821 and it was completed in 1838 at a cost of $16,677. Building probably began in 1829 when a plan for its foundations was drawn up; because of the marshy nature of the land it was built on a heavy framework of cross-timbering known as a 'grillage'.[13] It may have been this that dictated the tower's shape, for it is unique among martellos in being hexagonal.[14] It was built of brick, three storeys high and could accommodate fifty men; it supported a battery which was placed in front of it overlooking the lake. Strangely enough, two years after it was completed plans were drawn up for repairs and alterations; it was in service until at least 1892, in which year a return of its armament was made. It is still standing and is in a fair state of repair. It is used by its owner as a private camping and picnic site.[15] As well as its official name of Tower Dupré, it is also called Tower Philippon because it was built on land that originally belonged to Antoine Philippon junior. It is known, too, as Martello Castle, but purists would deny it the name martello for, despite the fact that it is one in intention, it breaks the fundamental rules of these buildings by having a low level entrance and no flat roof.

The second Louisiana tower was planned and built later at the southernmost point of Lake Borgne at Proctor's Landing or Proctorsville, about twenty miles from New Orleans. Its plans were put forward in 1845, at about the same time as those for the Key West martellos. It was rectangular in shape and supported a crescent shaped battery. Work was still going on at the outbreak of the civil war, for among the fortifications of the state an unfinished tower at Proctor's Landing was mentioned.

The final stage of the martello story was reached with the building of the towers at Key West in Florida. They were massive square structures placed diagonally inside large ramparts. Round the central tower were galleries and storehouses with casemate batteries beyond. The whole complex was a further break with tradition and the complete work was thought of and called a martello, not just the tower itself.

The Key West martellos were part of a scheme for the defence of the Gulf of Mexico and its northern coastline. When the American government realised the strategic importance of the island of Key West it decided to develop it as a naval base complete with a fort and four martellos. The purpose of the towers was to secure the main work, Fort Taylor, from enemy landings and the covering fire of the ships supporting them.[16] Sites for the four towers were selected in 1845, but it was not until 1861 that Captain Hunt was ordered to take possession of the land. Of the four towers planned, those on nearby Stock Island and Fleming Quay were never begun and work on the East and West Martellos went on slowly and without much enthusiasm until 1873 when it was abandoned. In the case of the West Martello, the tower itself was virtually complete but the battery was unfinished. The towers were of brick and possessed many of the characteristics of the original martellos—indeed, being square in plan they harked back to Captain Ford's proposals of 1803. They had the essential high-level entrance with a drawbridge, a central pillar and fine vaulted chambers. The pillar enclosed a spiral stair which led to the flat roof, in the parapet of which were machicola tions for firing downwards at the base of the tower.

The dimensions were:

height	36ft
length of wall at base	56ft
thickness of wall	8ft on seaward side
	5ft on landward side

As with many other martellos, these towers played a part in both World Wars; they were used as quarters for troops, signalling and lookout posts, and radio and anti-aircraft stations. West Martello was in a ruinous condition for many years and by 1950 only three rooms were left under the shelter of a roof. It had become a quarry for building materials and a playground for vandals owing to a long-standing dispute over the ownership of the land on which it stood. East Martello remained relatively sound but was deteriorating until 1950 when the Navy Department, to whom it had been handed over by the army six years before, declared it surplus to their requirements. A new era was about to begin for the martello. The Key West Art and Historical Society immediately took steps to preserve it, and in August of that year the tower was handed over to them. After an intensive cleaning and clearing up campaign, the building was opened to the public in December 1950. Since then, restoration work has been carried out and it has become an art gallery, museum and centre for cultural activities in a unique setting overlooking the sea.

Notes and references to this chapter appear on pages 166-7

CHAPTER TEN

THE END OF THE MARTELLO STORY

The end of martello building was not, of course, the end of their story. When the particular emergency for which they had been built was over, their subsequent history was one of abandonment by the military followed by neglect and decay whether they were built in the British Isles, South Africa or North America. The fact that, like the British tank traps and pillboxes of World War II, they were never put to the use for which they had been intended and that none of them ever fired a shot in anger, seems to have militated against them. In England they quickly became unpopular both with civilians and the army; as early as 1819 the Board of Ordnance sold some of them for building materials. As the nineteenth century progressed, they became outdated, as well as being outclassed by developments in artillery, in the testing of which at least three were destroyed in England. But Captain Ford had predicted in 1803, when he put forward his proposals for towers as sea-fortresses, that 'from the nature of their figure and substance, they will endure a great length of time'. He was quite correct. Many of those that survived time and tide and the vagaries of fashion have been put to various uses and each tower has its individual history.

In England, even before the Napoleonic wars were over, the martellos on the south coast were being used for purposes other than those for which they had been built. It was decided in January 1812 to put them to work as signalling stations. Naval and military messages were transmitted from Seaford in Sussex to Lympne in Kent by means of a union jack and three black canvas balls hoisted on a flagstaff mounted on the roof above the door. After 1820 this method gave way to semaphore machines erected on towers no 4, 27, 31 and 55. A similar method was used in Canada from the Duke of York's Tower until the advent of the telegraphic system. Another use found for them in England was as coastguard stations. A determined effort was made early in the nineteenth century to try to stamp out the traditional coastal occupation of smuggling, which was most prevalent on the coasts where the towers were. In Canada and Great Britain, before the towers were abandoned by the army, some became the homes of army pensioners and their families. The retired soldiers performed certain duties—mainly those connected with ventilating and trying to keep dry rot at bay—for the privilege of living in such strange, dark and damp buildings. It was not until the end of the century that some of the towers were freed by the army for civilian tenants and at about the same time the War Department began gradually to rid itself of the responsibility of tower upkeep by putting some up for sale.

Martello towers retained some military significance, however, in most places until the end of World War II. During the nineteenth century as political tensions built up in Europe, and England was threatened from across the Channel, they were once more called into service. When France produced her second revolution in 1830 and war and an invasion were anticipated, many of the towers were rearmed—or perhaps even armed for the first time—and some of the guns found on them in recent times were made in Carron in 1829. Such a one is the gun from the roof of no 13 at Hythe, which now stands outside the martello tower for all to see. Again, in 1845 when war with France was expected, the defensive qualities of martellos were assessed and the Duke of Wellington, then Prime Minister, visited the ones in Sussex in the Pevensey Bay vicinity and pronounced his verdict on them:

> There may be different opinions on the value of these towers as a defence. My own opinion is in their favour. At all events, if they are nothing else, each of them is an excellent defensive guard-house...

Along with dockyards and similar installations, martello towers were considered of sufficient importance to be omitted from the topographical detail when the relevant sheets of the 1in ordnance survey maps were reprinted during the 1870s, and this continued until the beginning of this century. Invasion scares occurred up to the 1940s and on each occasion the remaining martellos were brought into the scheme of coastal defence, but it was not until 1940 that they were really in the front-line. The preparations on the beaches at that time must have resembled those of the years when the martellos were built. Hitler, having produced a carbon copy of Napoleon's invasion plans, a watch was kept once more from the towers on the beaches and, for the first time, on the sky above them. Observation posts and range-finding equipment were erected on some of them while others had guns again on their one-time bomb-proof roofs; some were used as billets for troops or the local Home Guard. This was indeed the martello towers' swansong, and during this spell of active service many towers were scarred and shaken and one in Pevensey Bay was blown up by the enemy.

The uses for martellos in peace time have been varied and include dwellings, cafés, water towers and museums, the latter being perhaps the most appropriate and dignified. A movement for their preservation and restoration, begun at first by voluntary local effort and enthusiasm, has been growing slowly since 1925 when Murney Tower in Kingston, Ontario, was rescued by the town's historical society. Recently local authorities and relevant government departments have tentatively begun to take a hand in the work, except in the United States. Since 1950 the East Martello at Key West in Florida has been restored by the local historical society, while in Canada Fort Frederick Tower, the Prince of Wales Tower and the one at Saint John have all been restored by public bodies and are open to visitors. Ireland, too, has preserved an example of her martellos in the James Joyce Tower at Sandycove. The remaining South African tower at Simon's Town has been saved and, thanks to a sum of money set aside by the government in the 1970 defence estimates, further restoration work has been carried out and the interior is being fitted as a museum. This should be ready by March 1972 for the fiftieth anniversary celebrations of the South African navy. In England, home of the martello, public opinion has been slow in showing concern for this unique and comprehensive defence system. It was probably the publicity given to the attempted destruction of the Wish Tower at Eastbourne in 1959 that brought the historical significance of these buildings to the attention of a small section of people. Since then some progress has been made. Kent has been particularly fortunate. At Dymchurch no 24 has been entirely restored and no 25 repaired externally; soon no 23 will be as good as new and first-aid repairs are about to be carried out on no 1 at Folkestone.

For the rest, their fate may be destruction by the sea, demolition for road widening or building housing estates, or degradation among a sea of caravans. While they cannot be classed as gems of architecture, nothing is more appropriate than their stark simplicity in the flat landscapes where they occur, creating points of visual interest and giving a sense of scale with the skyline. Neither should their historical significance be disregarded, for they bear within themselves the very essence of the oldest masonry fortifications and have affinities with Phoenician watch-towers and early medieval castles. Wherever martellos survive, they stand as mute reminders of a completely different age of warfare and as a striking and unusual link between English speaking people and the roots of early western civilisation.

NOTES AND REFERENCES

Abbreviations used throughout:

PRO = Public Record Office
WO = War Office material at the PRO

1 INTRODUCTION

1 Many towers were built by the Genoese who were some of the great traders of the Mediterranean during the Middle Ages. In Corsica, which is directly south of Genoa, they built some eighty towers; they were so sited that the beacon fires on their roofs passed messages right round the island in a very short time as well as acting as a warning for people in the tower's immediate vicinity.

2 PRO/WO/33/25/1873.

3 THE EVOLUTION OF THE MARTELLO TOWER DESIGN

1 With regard to Jersey, this fact has been confirmed by Mrs Joan Stevens FSA, President of the Société Jersiase, who with Mr H. R. Pocock has supplied much of the information about this island. For Guernsey, Mr R. W. J. Payne, Honorary Secretary and Librarian of La Société Guernesiase, has confirmed the theory of the misnomer.

2 There is a tower very similar in design on the small island of Brehon, close to the island of Herm.

3 These are the dimensions of the tower at La Rocca.

4 PRO/WO/55/808 Report of Engineers Committee, 6 September 1787.

5 Details about the fort at Rocquaine, known as Chateau de Rocquaine or Fort Grey, were supplied by the Secretary of the Ancient Monuments Committee of Guernsey.

6 Details supplied by the Chairman of the Simon's Town Historical Society.

7 The Plan is at the PRO, reference MPH 712 (4).

8 Details from 'The Evolution of the Halifax Fortress, 1749-1928', Harry Piers, Publication No 7, Public Archives of Nova Scotia.

4 THE ENGLISH SOUTH COAST DEFENCES

1 Almost exactly the same plans with regard to evacuation were ready to be put into force if the need arose during World War I.

2 William Twiss (1745-1827) served for a number of years in Canada, becoming acting Commander Royal Engineers; on returning to England he was made Commanding Engineer of the Southern District.

3 PRO/WO/55/778, report from Brig-Gen William Twiss to Lieut-Gen Robert Morse, Inspector-General of Fortifications, dated Dover, 3 September 1804.

4 Entry dated 1 September 1823. Despite Cobbett's scathing remarks, the Germans took notice of the Royal Military Canal in their final invasion plans in 1940. The 7th Parachute Division was to be landed in the Lyminge-Hythe area and one of their orders was to open crossings over the canal at Hythe and to the west of it in front of the right wing of the 16th Army. From *Operation Sea Lion* by Ronald Wheatley.

5 Not many details are known of W. H. Ford's life. He was known as a practical joker, clever and amusing. Twiss was friendly with him and stayed at his house when on his tours. Ford became a Major-General and Lieut-Governor of the Royal Military Academy at Woolwich; he died 7 April 1829.

6 Ford's memorandum was written before July 1803 but the exact date is not known.

7 Sir David Dundas was in charge of the land forces in south and east England. It is interesting to note that serving under him were two officers who were well-acquainted with the towers at the Cape of Good Hope. They were Sir James Craig, commanding the troops north of the Thames in Essex and Suffolk and Francis Dundas who had succeeded him as acting governor of the Cape in 1798; he commanded the troops in Kent and Sussex. Undoubtedly they had some influence in the adoption of towers as a form of coastal defence.

8 PRO/WO/55/778.

9 The redoubts or circular forts consisted of an external wall against which were built barrack rooms, store rooms, etc, opening on to a circular open ground in the centre of the fort. The guns were mounted on the flat roof, and a moat 23ft wide and 35-40ft deep surrounded it. Some 50,000 bricks were said to have gone into a single course of the external walls. These forts are still standing at Dymchurch and Eastbourne; at the latter place, a model village is set up in the moat and in the fort itself is a 'Blue Grotto'. A similar fort was built at Harwich when the East Coast towers were constructed.

10 Traversing platforms came into use towards the end of the eigh-

teenth century; before this guns were turned by hand with pikes. The Mortella Point tower had such platforms at the time of the 1794 action.

11 PRO/WO/55/778, letter from Twiss to R. H. Crew Esq, Secretary to the Board of Ordnance; it was enclosed with the letter quoted on page 59 to Morse, asking him to 'forward or not, as you deem most proper'.

5 THE PLAN AND CONSTRUCTION OF THE ENGLISH MARTELLO TOWERS

1 PRO/WO/44/244 and WO/44/282.

2 From 'Martello Towers and the Defence of North East Essex in the Napoleonic Wars' by Kenneth Walker, published in the *Essex Review* no 47 (1958). However, Tower F at Clacton has base axes measuring 56ft and 57ft, while Seaford in Sussex, no 74, built to the South Coast tower design measures 48ft and 43ft.

3 Also from Kenneth Walker's 'Martello Towers and the Defence of North East Essex in the Napoleonic Wars'.

4 PRO/WO/55/778 Letter from Morse to Lieut-Colonel Hadden, Surveyor General to the Board of Ordnance.

5 John, 2nd Earl of Chatham, Master of Ordnance 1801-6.

6 See note 3.

7 Edward Hodges, 1762-1834—very few details of his life are known. A bust of him exists, in the possession of one of his descendants, Mr Lance Sieveking.

8 PRO/WO/55/778.

6 DISTRIBUTION OF THE SOUTH COAST TOWERS

1 From 'Defence Works in Britain, 1803 to 1805', by S. G. P. Ward, in *Journal of the Society for Army Historical Research.*

7 DISTRIBUTION OF THE EAST COAST TOWERS

1 Major-General John Moore, better known as Sir John Moore, the hero of Corunna.

2 Unlike the south-coast area evacuation plan, this time certain roads were to be kept open for the movement of troops only.

3 Also from 'Martello Towers and the Defence of North East Essex in the Napoleonic Wars', by Kenneth Walker.

4 PRO/WO/1/783 also 'Defence Works to Britain, 1803 to 1805,' by S. G. P. Ward, *Journal of the Society for Army Historical Research.*

8 IRELAND, JERSEY AND ORKNEY

1 Lord Cathcart, 1st Viscount and Earl, was General William Schaw Cathcart; his son was Commander-in-Chief in British North America from 1846 to 1849, at the time the Kingston martellos were

built and one of the towers was named after him.

2 PRO/WO/55/831 letter dated 8 January 1804 to Sir Charles Holloway, a Lieutenant-Colonel in the Royal Engineers.

3 From *The County and City of Cork Remembrancer or Annuals of the County and City of Cork,* Francis H. Tuckey 1837. The internal diameter of these batteries was nine times larger than that of the English martello towers.

4 PRO/WO/55/831, the quotations in this section are from this source.

5 Pigeon House, a coastal fort close to Dublin.

6 From *Romantic Inishowen* by G. H. P. Swan (1947).

7 This is a list of reported towers; some of them may, in fact, be martello towers, but this has not been confirmed. The first two in Galway Bay are marked on the map as ordnance towers; some of the others may be much older than martellos.

Galway Bay, a tower at Rosaveel
and at Golam Head
Shannon Estuary, a tower at Kilcredaun Head,
Doonaha,
Carrea Island,
and Doneen Point.
Tralee Bay, a tower at Rough Point.
Dingle Bay, a tower at Bray Head, Valentia Island which may be a signal station and two towers at Castlemaine Harbour.
Dingle Harbour, a tower at Reenbeg Point.
County Down, a tower near Ardglass.
Baltimore, a tower on Sherkin Island, but this is probably a signal station.
Crookhaven, a tower known as Caughlin's Tower.
Rack Island, two towers.
Ballyvoyle Head, near Dungarron, a tower in ruins, believed to have been a martello.

8 Quotations and some of the details from an article by H.R.S. Pocock on 'Jersey's Martello Towers' in *Sociétè Jersiase Annual Bulletin, 1971.*

9 THE NORTH AMERICAN MARTELLO TOWERS

1 From unpublished research material of George Munro.

2 Information from the Chief Reference Librarian, Halifax City Regional Library.

3 The title of the map is 'Plan of the Town and Fortifications of Quebec including the Works that are now carrying on to increase the Defence of the Place. Quebec, July 1808'.

4 Much of this material is taken from the brochure 'History of the Martello Tower' published by the New Brunswick Museum, a

reprint of an article in the *History Bulletin* of 1963 written by Dr George MacBeath, the former director of the museum.

5 WO/44/45, pages 415, 551 and 570.

6 This is a very ancient method of construction and was known to early Mediterranean civilisations; the Nuraghi, a tribe inhabiting Sardinia in about 1500BC, built the roofs of their dwellings in this way but without mortar and the central stone can be lifted out, as with the Kingston martellos.

7 Much of the information is from a booklet *A Short History of Kingston as a Military and Naval Centre* by G. F. G. Stanley and Richard A. Preston, Department of History, Royal Military College.

8 From a pamphlet, *A story in Stone—Murney Tower* by W. S. Lovell, revised by Richard A. Preston.

9 Some of this material was supplied by Mr E. R. Lewis, author of *Seacoast Fortifications of the United States.*

10 National Archives and Records Service, Washington DC Drawer 64 Sheet 9 and Drawer 64 Sheet 31. The Director of the Cartographic Records Division and his staff have done sterling work in unearthing a considerable number of maps, plans and sections, many of which had probably not seen the light of day for at least a century.

11 National Archives Drawer 68 Sheet 3.

12 National Archives Drawer 133 Sheet 22.

13 National Archives Drawer 87 Sheet 7.

14 National Archives Drawer 255 Sheet 13 and Drawer 87 Sheet 12.

15 From Mrs L. Kaltenburgh.

16 Some of this material is from the booklet *The Martello Towers and the Story of Key West,* (1951) Publicity Committee of the Key West Art and Historical Society.

BIBLIOGRAPHY

No books have been published on the subject of martello towers, and material for further reading is therefore scarce. Listed below are the articles and pamphlets available. For the rest, the sources of this book are at the Public Record Office and these are given in the notes and references for the relevant chapters, as well as answers to my queries from those who have been kind enough to deal with these and who are thanked in the long list of acknowledgements. Some local newspaper cuttings have been of interest and there are references to the towers in certain guide books. Local archives collections also have papers on the subject on which some work remains to be done; they deal almost exclusively with the appropriation of land on which to build the towers. The list is divided into European, South African and North American sections so that it is easier to follow; the background history reading naturally overlaps in most cases.

EUROPE

For political history of the period

The Cambridge History of the British Empire, Vols 5 and 6 (1930)

For detailed accounts of military and naval incidents

Fortescue, The Hon J. W., LL D. *History of the British Army*, Vols 4 and 5 (1921)

For a detailed survey of invasion plans

Fleming, Peter. *Invasion 1940* (1957)

Richmond, Admiral Sir Herbert W., KGB, DCL. *The Invasion of Britain.* An account of plans, attempts and countermeasures 1586-1918 (1941)

Wheatley, Ronald. *Operation Sea Lion* (1958)

For general reading there are references to martellos in

Joyce, James. *Ulysses* (new edition, 1960), 1-28

Lindley, Kenneth. *Coastline* (1967)

Quite indispensible and the inspiration of this book

Mead, Commander Hilary P., RN, 'The Martello Towers of England' *Mariner's Mirror* (Journal of the Society for Nautical Research) Vol 34 (1948), 205-17, 294-303

For detailed accounts of defence works and valuable references to War Office papers in the Public Record Office

Ward, S. G. P., 'Defence Works of Britain, 1803-1805', *Journal of the Society for Army Historical Research,* Vol 27 (1949)

For accounts of individual towers or groups of them

Ellman, Richard. *James Joyce's Tower.* Published and issued by the Eastern Regional Tourism Organisation Limited, Dublin (1969)

Lemon, Lt-Col C. H., DSO, 'The Story of the Martello Tower', *Rye Museum News Letter* 10 (September, 1961). Privately produced

Piper, John. 'Martello Towers', *The House of Whitbread Magazine,* Vol 18 no 1 (1958), 12-15

Walker, Kenneth. 'Martello Towers and the Defence of North East Essex in the Napoleonic Wars'. *Essex Review,* 47 (1958), 171-185

Ward, Ronald, FRIBA. *The Martello Tower, Hythe* (1968). Privately produced

SOUTH AFRICA

United States Naval Institute Proceedings, 86 no 11, 1960, 107-8; letter from H. C. Willis, Chairman of Simon's Town Historical Society.

NORTH AMERICA

For the political history

Graham, Gerald S. *A Concise History of Canada* (1967)

Morison, Samuel Eliot. *The Oxford History of the American People* (1965)

Wellman, Paul I. *The House Divides* (1966)

Canada: the Canadian martellos are well documented and apart from the articles and brochures listed below, there are brochures for towers which are open to the public.

Fergusson, Dr Charles Bruce, 'The Martello Tower at Halifax', *The Dalhousie Report*, 43 no 2 (1963), 212-19

Munro, George. *The Prince of Wales Tower* unpublished historical research report

Piers, Harry. 'The Evolution of the Halifax Fortress 1749-1928' Publication No 7, *Public Archives of Nova Scotia* (1947)

Roy, P. G. 'Les Tours Martello à Québec', *Bulletin de Recherches Historiques,* 566 (1936)

Stanley, George F. G. and Preston, Richard A. *'A Short History of Kingston as a Military and Naval Centre'*, revised edition of a booklet published in 1950.

United States Naval Institute Proceedings, 84 no 12 (1958), 121-2, a letter on the Kingston, Ontario martello towers. 84 no 11 (1960), 108, a letter on the Saint John, New Brunswick martello tower.

United States of America: very little has been published on the subject of martello towers.

Lewis, E. R. *Seacoast Fortifications of the United States* (Newton Abbot, 1970), 41-2

The Publicity Committee of the Key West Art and Historical Society, *'The Martello Towers and the Story of Key West'* (1951)

United States Naval Institute Proceedings, 85 no 10 (1959), 100-1, two letters on martello towers in America

ACKNOWLEDGEMENTS

Transcripts of Crown copyright records in the Public Record Office appear by permission of the Controller of Her Majesty's Stationery Office.

I have to thank a great many people who, in an official capacity or as private individuals, have helped me in my research and have shown interest in the work as well as giving me encouragement in the enterprise. The list is long and formidable and my gratitude to them all is sincere; without their assistance this book could not have been undertaken and I hope they will regard it as a joint venture. I have divided the list geographically so that it is not too unwieldy

ENGLAND

The Keeper of Books and Archives and the Library Research Assistant at the National Maritime Museum, Greenwich; the Assistant Inspector of Ancient Monuments at the Ministry of Public Building and Works; the Librarian of the Royal Commission on Historical Monuments; Major R. G. Bartelot of the Royal Artillery Institution, Woolwich, and the members of Operation Seashore, particularly Anthony Smith and Douglas Botting.

The Inspector, South Eastern Division of HM Coastguard; Captain M. J. Button, RN, HMS *Ganges*; the Area Officer of the Ministry of Public Building and Works, Shorncliffe; the Clerk of Kent County Council; the Clerks of the Councils of the Borough of Aldeburgh, the County Borough of Eastbourne, Felixstowe, Clacton Urban District Council, Seaford Urban District Council, the Borough of Rye, and the Town Clerk of Folkestone. The County Planning Officers of Essex, East Suffolk and East Sussex County Councils; the Engineer and Surveyor of the Romney Marsh Rural District Council. The Librarians of the County Borough of Eastbourne and the County Library, Chelmsford; the Curator of the Towner Art Gallery and Museum, Eastbourne, and the Honorary Curator of Rye Museum; the County Archivist of Essex County Council. The Camp General Manager, Butlin's Holiday Camp, Clacton-on-Sea, and Messrs Whitbread & Co Ltd.

R. Romilly Fedden, John D. Floydd, ARIBA, Sir Geoffrey Harmsworth, Bart, FSA, H. Hooker, Miss M. A. Huxley, JP, MA, the Revd Nigel O'Connor, Mrs P. Osborne and her two accomplices, E. W. Parker, Lance Sieveking, Mr and Mrs R. E. Stone, Kenneth Walker and Ronald Ward, FRIBA.

IRELAND

The Irish Embassy in London; the Assistant Director, Ordnance Survey, Dublin, and the Office of Public Works, Dublin. The Curator of the Joyce Museum; John de Courcy Ireland PhD, Honorary Research Officer, Maritime Institute of Ireland; Valentine E. Kirwan, P. O'Keeffe, E. C. Robinson, and Miss Tombe.

NORTHERN IRELAND

The Humanities Librarian, Local History Department, Belfast Central Library.

THE CHANNEL ISLES

Guernsey: The Secretary of the Ancient Monuments Committee; the Honorary Secretary and Librarian, La Société Guernesiase; Victor Coysh, the Guernsey Press.

Jersey: The Local History Librarian, Central Library; Mrs Joan Stevens, FSA, President, Société Jersiase, and H. R. S. Pocock.

ORKNEY

Ernest W. Marwick, Kirkwall.

SOUTH AFRICA

The Information Attaché, South African Embassy in London. The Chairman of the Simon's Town Historical Society.

CANADA

The High Commissioner for Canada in London; the Department of Indian Affairs and Northern Development, Historical Research, National Historic Sites Service and the Regional Director, Atlantic Region of the National and Historic Parks Branch. The Director of the Directorate of History, Canadian Forces Headquarters; Archiviste, Section Cartes et Gravures, Archives Nationales du Québec. Three members of the staff of the Royal Military College at Kingston—the Commandant, the Information Officer and the Curator of the College Museum at Fort Frederick; the President of the Kingston Historical Society. The Chief Reference Librarian of Halifax City Regional Library and the Secretary of the Martello Tower, New Brunswick Museum.

UNITED STATES OF AMERICA

The Embassy of the United States of America in London; the Assistant Librarian of the Navy Department Library; the USA General Services Administration, National Archives and Records Service, Cartographic Records Division; the Editor of the United States Naval Institute Proceedings; the Associate Curator, Division of Naval History, Smithsonian Institution; the Director of the American Association for State and Local History. The Head of the Louisiana Division, City of New Orleans Public Library; the Director of the Charleston Museum. Mrs Louise P. Kaltenburgh, E. R. Lewis and Mrs Oliver Rutledge.

INDEX

Abbreviations:

Ex = Essex, Suf = Suffolk, Sx = Sussex,
CI = Channel Isles, Jy = Jersey,
Gu = Guernsey, Ire = Ireland,
NB = New Brunswick, NS = Nova Scotia,
Ont = Ontario, SA = South Africa,
USA, Ga = Georgia, Fa = Florida,
SC = South Carolina, La = Louisiana.

Illustrations are indicated by figures in italics